MY LOVE IS FREE...

But the Rest of Me Don't Come Cheap

P. S. WALL

Ballantine Books • New York

A Ballantine Book
Published by The Ballantine Publishing Group

These stories originally appeared in P. S. Wall's syndicated column, "Off the Wall."

http://www.randomhouse.com

Library of Congress Catalog Card Number: 98-96868

ISBN 0-345-42887-0

This edition published by arrangement with Rutledge Hill Press, 211 Seventh Avenue North, Nashville, TN 37219.

Manufactured in the United States of America

Cover design by Kristine V. Mills-Noble
Cover photo by Robert Pierce

First Ballantine Books Edition: January 1999

10 9 8 7 6 5 4 3 2 1

For Sweetie

CONTENTS

ACKNOWLEDGMENTS

Mom, Dad, Llewellyn, and Cortney, thanks for being the best cheering section a girl could have

My Mountain Man

WHEN I FIRST MET MY SWEETIE, HE WASN'T exactly what you'd call the "outdoor type." His idea of untamed territory was that thin stretch of grass between parking lanes at the mall.

So, the first year I took him on our annual hike up Mount LeConte, the rest of the gang was a bit leery.

"He's a music major?" Butch asks, as he cleans his knife on his jeans.

"You got a problem with that?" I say.

"All I'm sayin' is, the boy looks a little frail."

"Butch," I say, eyes narrowed, "don't make me hurt you."

It's not like we just crash landed in the Andes. We're in the Smokies, for Pete's sake. Take a wrong turn and you're at Ripley's Believe It or Not.

"O.K. Sweetie," I say, as I slather 50 SPF on his lily-white face, "how're we doing?"

"So, tell me again why we're climbing a mountain to stay in an unheated cabin with no running water?" Sweetie asks.

Fortunately, a mockingbird suddenly bursts into song. Transfixed, Sweetie is drawn to it like Sylvester to Tweety Bird. While I load up our backpacks, he's warbling up at the tree, trying to sing harmony with the blasted bird.

The route we're taking is about a six-hour climb, if you

linger at lunch and stop for photos. I have serious doubts
Sweetie has spent six consecutive hours in sunlight in his life,
unless it was for the opera festival at Spoleto.

When we get to the creek, Butch decides we should
leapfrog it instead of taking the bridge. The water is liquid
ice. Jumping from rock to rock is like dancing on ice cubes.
I'm so preoccupied with my feet, I only look up in time to
see Sweetie, arms out like wings and toes pointed, gracefully
leaping from rock to rock like a gazelle. As he takes the final
jump, a good five feet to shore, the rest of us teeter in the
frothing water with mouths open.

"How'd he do that?" Butch yells back at me.

"Dance lessons," I yell. "He's got legs like rocket boosters."

Cold and wet, we collapse for lunch. While the rest of us
try to get the feeling back in our toes, Sweetie scales a ninety-
degree rock wall to get a better vista—using only his fingertips.

"How is he doing that?" Butch asks, as we watch Sweetie
smear on ChapStick while dangling from three fingers.

"Piano lessons," I sigh. "He's got fingers that can crack
walnuts."

The last stretch of the climb is always the hardest. The air
is thin, and my calves start to cramp. While the rest of us
trudge up the trail, Sweetie is fifty feet ahead, singing high-
lights from *The Barber of Seville*.

"How's he doing that?" Butch wheezes.

"Voice lessons," I gasp. "He's got lungs like a beluga whale."

"Look!" Butch shouts, unable to suppress his rage any
longer, "just because he's got great hands and endurance like the
Energizer Bunny, doesn't make him a better man than me!"

"Butch . . . Butch," I say, gently patting him on the shoulder, "of course it does."

You were thinking women throw themselves at musicians
because they appreciate the arts?

Subtle

APPARENTLY CERTAIN WOMEN ATTRACT CERtain types of men. I always seem to get the subtle ones.

So, I'm sitting in a substitute dentist's chair with a chipped tooth. My usual dentist is at Club Med wearing beads and sipping piña coladas out of coconuts, compliments of my last gum surgery, thank you.

I must say it strikes me as a bit odd when the substitute dentist tells his assistant to take her lunch break at 9 A.M., but when it comes to dentists, go figure. I mean we're talking about a man whose livelihood comes from making people spit blood, right?

"Open," the substitute dentist says, leaning over me.

As always, just about the time he has his hand, two instruments, and a few toes in my mouth, he starts making casual conversation. Evidently they teach this in dental school.

"You don't remember me, do you?" he asks.

Under the circumstances I wouldn't recognize Elvis. Just the same, this guy does not look the least bit familiar.

"I sat next to you in Animal Physiology in college," he says.

"Eeeeelllly?" I say, wondering which of the two times I failed it he's referring to.

This may also explain why I don't recognize him. Cute,

clean-cut, future doctor . . . none of the qualities I was looking for in a guy back then.

"Actually," he says, "I asked you out."

"Oooo id?" I say.

He shakes his head and chuckles. "Your standing me up was
probably one of the most humiliating moments of my life."

Then he smiles at me, sticks a buzzing drill in my mouth,
and says, "Let me know if this hurts."

Now, I would never have stood this guy up. I was never
your "stand them up" kind of girl. I was more your "grab them
by the knees if they run" type.

I figure this guy must have been too subtle for me to know
he was asking me out. Forgive me if I failed to realize that
"Would you like to watch me dissect a pig?" really meant,
"You are the soulmate of my life. Come spend eternity in my
arms." I guess I'm just a little slow in these matters.

Fortunately, I didn't have this problem with Sweetie. He
didn't ask me out subtly—he didn't ask me out at all. I
waited with baited breath for almost six months for some in-
dication that this guy knew I was alive. I took no chances—if
he twitched I jumped.

"Excuse me," I said, "but I couldn't help but notice you
just twitched. Was that like a *real* twitch, or did you perhaps
have something else in mind?"

Heading into the second season of real twitches I decided
I'd better take this bull by the horns before some other cow
moved into the pasture. So, I drove thirty miles over hills and
dales and creeks without bridges, stopping once for gas and
twice for directions, to Sweetie's cabin.

"Hi," I said when he opened the door. "I just happened to
be in the neighborhood with this Bundt cake . . ."

I was going to bake a pie, but I figured that would have
been way too obvious.

The Runaway

Y ESTERDAY, ROSIE'S HUSBAND RAN AWAY FROM home. He said he was going to the dentist, which wasn't a complete lie. He did swing by the clinic and pick up the twenty-four-year-old hygienist on his way out of town.

"It's just a phase he's going through," Mindy says, surveying a platter of pastries. "Are these homemade?"

"Men are scum," Leila says, sipping fruit tea with a sprig of fresh mint.

We're sitting around Rosie's kitchen table and the atmosphere is a combination of wake-slash-brunch. The melon balls look like they've been sized with a compass and the seashell-blue napkins are folded into origami swans. Even in her hour of despair, Rosie makes the average woman look like a cave dweller.

"I never saw it coming," Rosie says, as she lifts my feet off the chair and slides a newspaper under them.

"The wife is always the last to know," Mindy says, licking her cream cheese mustache.

"Men are dirt balls," Leila says, her finger on her chin as she deliberates between a sausage ball and a ham-and-Brie croissant.

I know I should say something supportive, but at the moment I'm transfixed with my reflection in Rosie's linoleum.

"It's no-wax," Rosie says, "but I find hand-rubbing with a dab of car polish really brings out the luster."

To each her own, but the day I get down on my hands and knees to buff a no-wax floor, shoot me.

"He'll be back," Mindy assures her.

"He took all his things," Rosie says, as she sucks crumbs off the table using a tiny little Dustbuster.

Looking around, I try to figure out exactly what "things" she's referring to. Nothing seems to be missing. In fact, there's no evidence a man has ever set foot in the place, except for a grease spot on the left side of the two-car garage.

"Do you ever think Sweetie might leave you?" Rosie asks, snipping a wayward petal off the flower arrangement.

Leila and Mindy gasp, then quickly genuflect to guard against twenty-four-year-old spirits with perfect teeth.

"Men are like wild animals," I say. "Some domesticate more easily than others."

The truth is, Sweetie may eat out of my hand every now and then, but whenever I hear him scratching at the front door to get in, I consider it a miracle.

"Where did I go wrong?" Rosie sighs, as she mists the ferns above the sink.

Rosie's husband always looked like a wolf in a pet store window. I honestly think he tried to stick it out. But somehow you knew it was just a matter of time before the PLEASE PUT THE LID DOWN sign would send him howling back to the wilderness.

This does not mean, however, if he were my husband, I wouldn't track him down and skin him and his little twenty-four-year-old plaque remover.

"Maybe I'll get a dog," Rosie says.

"Poodles are nice," Mindy nods. "They don't shed . . ."

". . . and there's very little body odor," Leila adds.

Some women run with wolves, but the majority would be much happier with your basic lap dog.

At the Cosmetics Counter

THE BAG BOY THOUGHT I WAS MY YOUNGER SIS-
ter's mother today. He casually dropped this bit of napalm in
between his impersonation of Christian Slater pushing a grocery cart and fascinating facts about music groups that are
three seconds old.

"Like . . . your mom looks almost young enough to be
your sister," he said to my sister, as he slung a bag of cans on
top of my tomatoes.

Like . . . why doesn't he just drive a stake through my heart?

Under normal circumstances I wouldn't trust this boy to
know the difference between paper and plastic, but when it
comes to looks or age, he has the only credential required:
"Male—sexual preference irrelevant."

With that one sentence he sucked the youth right out of
me. I could feel my skin tightening on my cheekbones like
wet leather drying on a wood block. Suddenly my breasts
dropped to my butt, my butt dropped to my knees, and I
have no idea where my knees went. By that time my joints
were so stiff, I couldn't bend over to look.

After I stopped hyperventilating, I reviewed. I am the
same age as Michelle Pfeiffer and Sharon Stone. I am a little
younger than Kim Basinger. I'm a lot younger than Raquel

Welch. Oh wait, Raquel Welch is no good. I dropped out of the womb with less skin tone than she has at fifty-whatever.

Anyway, would the bag boy have called Michelle Pfeiffer "Mom"? I think not. Hollywood women never age. It's all attitude, I tell you. Attitude, and, of course, makeup.

If you hurry you can still see my skid marks in front of the cosmetics counter at the mall.

"May I help you?" the flawless, young salesgirl asks.

"I want to look like Isabella Rossellini," I say, gasping for breath.

"Of course you do," she says empathetically. This woman is so cool I doubt she has sweat glands. Of course, she can afford to be gracious; she hasn't recently been turned into a geriatric shar-pei by an evil, youth-sucking bag boy.

"You must have seen the picture in Sunday's paper of Isabella and her twin," she says, analytically turning my face from side to side with a tongue depressor.

Slapping the clipping onto the counter in front of me, she goes for supplies.

"Wow," I say, as I stare down at the newspaper article. "Isabella looks at least ten years younger than her sister."

"It's all attitude," the saleswoman says knowingly, "and, of course—makeup."

Thirty minutes and 250 bucks later I have both. There's night cream and day cream, eye cream and lip cream. There's a tiny bottle of oil that cost more per ounce than plutonium. I've got your peel, your scrub, and your makeup with a sunscreen that an atomic blast couldn't penetrate.

I walk out of that mall a new woman, looking good, feeling good. Confident that the aging process has not only stopped, but that time is peeling off my face like the pages of a calendar being blown backward by jet exhaust.

Sweetie notices something is different immediately.

"Oh, it's nothing really," I purr nonchalantly. "Just a new moisturizer."

"It smells kind of funny," he says, taking a step back.

"Funny?"

My mind flips through the possible ingredients that might be the cause. Collagen . . . placenta . . . avocado . . . apricot pits . . . and I'm pretty sure something that comes from a sheep.

"Maybe urea?" I ask, speed-reading the ingredients off the box.

"Urea? Isn't that like . . . pee?"

I've got all my new cosmetics packed in a box, ready to send to my mother. For now I think I'll just work on the attitude part. At the moment it reeks of urea too, but what are you gonna do?

The Appointment

I WAS BROUGHT UP TO BELIEVE THAT THE ONLY thing a doctor is good for is alimony.

"We're not moving until you put your seatbelt on," I say, slamming the car into PARK.

I've been sitting in the driveway for fifteen minutes, trying to coerce my great-aunt into a little civil obedience. It's like trying to get a cat to fetch.

Chin up and jaw set, Aunt May stares out the window and pretends I don't exist.

"It's chilly in here," Aunt May says, shivering as she pulls her full-length fur around her.

Actually, it's so hot inside my car you could fuse glass. Furthermore, someone really needs to study the chemical reaction between *Evening in Paris* and mothballs. I'm fairly certain it produces some kind of hallucinogen.

"Why won't you put your seatbelt on?" I ask, cracking the window.

"If you start to crash," Aunt May says, "I want to be able to jump out of this thing."

Aunt May snaps open her pocketbook and takes out her Ponds translucent.

"In 1937, Mr. Charles Martin's brakes failed him, and he crashed right into the pavilion at Union Station," Aunt May says, as she powders her nose. "I jumped out and never got a scratch."

"What happened to Mr. Martin?" I ask.

"He married the Sullivan girl," Aunt May says, snapping her compact closed. "The one with a bald spot."

Aunt May turns to face me. She looks as if someone hit her in the face with a bag of Pillsbury Self-Rising.

"I will say this for her," Aunt May says. "She wore the snappiest hats."

I've died and gone to Kabuki theater.

"If you don't fasten your seatbelt," I say, "we're going to be late for your appointment."

"I haven't let a doctor touch me in sixty years!" Aunt May snaps.

"Don't worry, Dr. Felts is gay."

"I don't care how cheerful he is!" Aunt May says. "I don't intend to spend my last hours tied to tubes!"

"Aunt May, it's an eye exam."

It finally occurred to us that Aunt May needed glasses the day we found her watering her plastic plants. By that time, she had accumulated fourteen cats—all named Rhett Butler—and had filled her neighbor's Jeep Cherokee with compost while they were on vacation in Europe.

"I don't need glasses!" Aunt May declares.

"Fine. Don't wear them."

"Only old maids wear glasses," she grumbles.

"What do old mules wear?" I mutter.

"Emma Lee, how dare you use that tone with me!"

"Aunt May," I say, "I'm Paula."

Squinting, Aunt May leans into my face and inspects me

like a bug. Ponds powder floods up my nose. Choking, I let out a little cough.

"Well," Aunt May sniffs, dropping back onto her side of the car, "you will never be the beauty your mother was."

"You think I'm ugly now," I say as I buckle her seatbelt on. "Wait until you get glasses."

Girls' Night Out

S₀, I TOLD HIM, EITHER HE STARTS SHOWING
me some affection—or ELSE!" Maxine says, stabbing the air
with her finger like Saddam Hussein.

Well, I'm sure that put her husband in the mood.

Here's the rub—or lack of it, as it were. The more women
demand attention, the less men give it to us. The less we get,
the meaner we become. Until finally, one day, we turn into
men. And then, unless you're married to a gay guy, you're really out of luck.

"WAITER!!!," Maxine barks across the coffee shop, "DO
WE LOOK DEAD OVER HERE?!"

In Maxine's case, we fear the transformation has already
begun.

It's girls' night out, or as Sweetie refers to it, my Hor-
moaning Support Group.

We women, on the other hand, think of it as that precious
time when we come together for consciousness raising and
intellectual enhancement.

We just saw the movie *Tin Cup* with Kevin Costner and
Don Johnson, and while the ushers are cleaning our slobber off
the screen with a squeegee, we're chowing down on espresso
and cheesecake at our favorite haunt, The Bottomless Pit.

"I bet Melanie Griffith never had to beg Don for attention," Chrisy says, sipping her latté.

The problem with romantic movies is, they bring to light how UN-romantic your own life has become.

"You just would not believe the things I have to do . . ." Leila mutters into her Café Carmel.

"Will you please explain to me, why you can't keep a man off of you before marriage, and you can't keep him off the couch after?!" Maxine growls, as our waiter refills her cup.

"Honest, sir, I've never met your husband," he stutters, as he backs away from our table.

"So, the other night," Chrisy says, "I light the candles, put on the music and walk out wearing nothing but a ruby red teddy and *Chanel No. 5.*"

"Yeah . . ." we say, mouths full of cheesecake.

"He said I looked like Miss Kitty and laughed so hard he got the hiccups."

Moaning, we all wither into our chairs.

It's not like we don't try to keep the fires burning. It just seems like our matches have gotten a little damp.

". . . I just cannot believe the things I've done . . ." Leila mumbles.

"I ask you," Maxine says, her voice cracking into a resonating baritone, "what's a girl to do?"

Besides lose forty pounds and wash the pabulum off her muumuu, I'm at a loss.

"You know," I say, "my grandfather was still chasing my grandmother around the house after fifty years of marriage."

"They just don't make men like they used to," Maxine says, picking her teeth with her stir stick.

"What was her secret?" Chrisy asks.

"I don't know," I say, shaking my head. "She was always slapping him off of her. They slept in separate bedrooms. I bet he never once saw her naked. Seems like the more she pushed him away, the more he . . ."

A silence falls over the group. Slowly, a ray of white light spotlights our faces and a choir of silver-haired grandmother angels, with wings and practical shoes, sings, "Come on baby, light my fire . . ."

"The old ones were so wise," Chrisy sighs.

"We have much to learn," Leila agrees.

We glance over at Maxine. Loosening her belt, she lets out a belch.

Ya Want Fries with That?

～⁓

Iℕ ORDER TO SNAG A MAN YOU HAVE TO HAVE
at least one of the three qualities men look for in a woman:
looks, cooks, or old money.

I personally am fluent in four cuisines and can do things
with a potato that will make a man weep.

Fifteen seconds after meeting Sweetie I knew that boy
was exactly what I wanted under my Christmas tree, so I
scurried home and started combing the culinary. When a
wind from the East blew Betty Crocker open to the chapter
on soufflés, I threw back my head and cackled.

"Yes!" I said to my Cuisinart. "Exotic, yet familiar. Basic,
yet with a touch of finesse."

I spent two days shopping, chopping, whipping, and grat-
ing, and at exactly forty-five minutes before my future prince
was to arrive, I slipped that sucker into the oven.

I don't mean to brag or anything, but never in the history
of cooking has there ever been a more perfect soufflé. If
Michelangelo had cooked instead of painted, this soufflé
would have been his Sistine Chapel. I'm talking, hang up the
apron, Julia Child.

My chest swollen with pride—and a little help from Play-
tex—I place the dish in front of him.

"What is it?" Sweetie asks skeptically.

"Chicken soufflé," I beam.

"Yeah? What's in it?"

"Organically grown, hormone-free breast of chicken, handpicked mushrooms, three cheeses, coarse ground pepper, and fresh scallions. I gathered the eggs myself—and churned the butter," I say, blushing modestly.

He stares down at the plate.

"It smells like buzzard armpits," he says, crinkling his nose. "Got any bologna?"

Now, let's review the multitude of mistakes made on this occasion.

Chances are the minute *soufflé* left my lips, the boy's teeth clamped together like a stainless steel bear trap. Men want their foods to sound American.

Sweetie would just as soon starve to death as eat something called Porc Saucisse de Fumeé. But call it smoked sausage, and he'll have that head tilted back and mouth open like a baby bird.

I now keep a Rolodex in my kitchen with alternative names for foods. Pork Teriyaki—pig fingers. Croissants—twisty bread. Manicotti—BIG macaroni and cheese.

Another mistake I made was telling him what was in the soufflé. Men don't really want to know what they're eating. Anything over two ingredients and the muscles in their throats start to contract.

"What's that?" Sweetie asks.

"Consommé," I say.

"*Con-som-mé*," he repeats, narrowing his eyes. "You're not puttin' THAT in the soup are you?"

"No! No, of course not," I say. "It's for the dog."

"Good," he says, relaxing. "Mother never put *consommé* in her soup."

Sweetie continues to think about this, then adds, "Are you sure it's O.K. to give it to the dog?"

"Well, I won't if you don't want me to, sweetheart."

"Maybe you better not," he says, flexing his masculine authority.

"O.K. my darling," I say, smiling.

As soon as he's out the door I pour the consommé in the pot, and life goes on.

Probably the biggest mistake a woman can make is trying to force a man to eat something he doesn't want to eat. I learned this the hard way. It's not something I like to talk about, but I will tell you it involved a squash casserole and explains why Sweetie has a little fork-shaped scar on his upper lip.

I was one of the fortunate few who got a second chance. The next meal I fixed Sweetie was a hamburger steak with cheese and onions, garlic bread, and frozen fries. I cooked the whole mess in fifteen minutes with one pan and a spatula.

Sweetie said it was the best meal he'd ever had, and there was love in his eyes as he said it.

Betting on Virginity

$\sim$

I T'S MY FIRST TIME AT THE HORSE TRACK, AND I must admit I don't see the big deal. The men are pint-sized and they're wearing silk. It's like thumbing through a Victoria's Secret catalog for Keebler Elves.

Knowing my penchant for risk taking, I have a fifty tucked in my pocket—enough for five two-dollar bets, a snack, and a sweatshirt for Sweetie. While I'm standing in line trying to decipher my schedule, I notice a shadow fall over me from behind.

"Par-don," a dark voice says.

I look back over my shoulder and there stands Lawrence of Arabia, fully regaled in white robe, headgear, and Italian shoes.

"I rub your golden hair," Lawrence says, with an accent dripping crude oil.

Now, I'm not one of those girls who's been waiting for her sheikh to come in. I'm a one-Sweetie girl, so I give the stranger my most polite "eat sand and die" look.

"No, no," Lawrence insists, waving ten pounds of gold and diamond rings. "You virgin? Yes?"

I'm still rolling this one over, when the nun in line in front of me says, "It's your first time at the track, dear. He thinks your blonde hair will bring him luck."

Clairol should put this on their box.

"Our Middle Eastern friends have such peculiar ideas," the nun smiles. "By the way, dear, would you mind kissing this five-er?"

For the sake of international goodwill, I decide to be gracious with my virginity.

"Many thanks," Lawrence says, bowing.

"Sure thing," I say, hoping Sister Secretariat didn't notice my lips didn't actually make contact with her five dollar bill. God only knows where that bill's been.

Lawrence motions with his hand, and a strange bug-eyed man appears, his arms wrapped around a leather briefcase like it's a life preserver. Lawrence snaps his fingers and I'm expecting this guy to snatch a fly out of the air and pop it into his mouth. Instead, he opens the briefcase and pulls out a wad of bills.

"You make bet for me," Lawrence says, handing me his money.

Apparently, it makes no difference to Lawrence that my bet is based solely on the fact that I find pale magenta silk on a gray-flannel horse an appealing color motif.

While the lady at the betting booth counts out his money, I count along. All I can say is, if this is his idea of money to burn, thank goodness it hasn't occurred to him to run for president.

I hand Lawrence his ticket, and catching the fever, decide to blow my whole allotted ten bucks on this one race.

It's a clear and balmy day at Arlington. The grass looks like it's been manicured with a Remington razor, and flags, every color in the economy box of Crayola crayons, curl and snap in the breeze. The horses, restless, paw the ground and snort as the Keebler Elves try to hold them in the gate.

The gun goes off and . . . I'm just getting in the mood when the whole thing is over. Talk about déjà vu all over again.

Lawrence's little bug-eyed friend is already at the window when I go to collect my winnings. Neatly tucking eight stacks of bills into his briefcase, he snubs me like I'm last year's model and scurries off into the crowd.

I'm trying to decide whether or not to roll my original ten over on the next race, when I notice a small shadow fall across my knees.

"Most beautiful blonde hair," a Japanese man says, bowing.

"You can touch it if you want to," I say, bowing back, "but I lost my virginity on the last race."

"No matter to me," he says, smiling. "I like horse with experience."

Casting Off

R ETIREMENT IS LIKE SEX. MEN LOVE TO TALK about it, but when the time finally comes, they're good for about fifteen minutes, then they're dying to put their ties back on.

It is 5:30 A.M. and I'm propped on a life preserver in a fishing boat. I have a fishing rod between my knees and a mug of coffee in my hands. I'm assuming my hook is in the water. The fog is so thick, for all I know the boat could still be resting on the trailer in the parking lot.

"Sure is foggy," I say.

"You gonna talk, or you gonna fish?" J.D. snaps from somewhere in front of me.

After thirty-five years of planning, dreaming, and talking of nothing else, J.D. retired two months ago. He did not go gently. The company finally threw him a surprise retirement party and changed the locks on the doors.

There's a frantic whir up ahead as J.D. reels in his line to check his bait again. I should probably pull mine up, if for no other reason than to see if it's wet. But I'm thinking, why spoil a perfectly good morning with movement?

"You want a sandwich?" I ask, feeling inside the cooler of food my aunt fixed for us.

"What kind?" J.D. asks.

I take a bite. Then I take another bite. Either it's a sushi sandwich or I'm eating our bait. Aunt Midge is a gourmet cook, which means, when you go to dinner at J.D.'s and Midge's, you ransack McDonald's on the way home. I'm guessing the sandwiches are anchovies and deviled eggs left over from her bridge game.

Having supped on recycled finger food the night before, J.D. opts for the Breakfast of Champions. The sound of a top popping is followed by spilling foam and the slurp of rapid chugging.

It came as quite a surprise to J.D. that the company did not crash and burn without him. For weeks he watched the Dow, convinced the company's stock was going to plummet. The day the stock ticked up two points, J.D. bought a brand new fishing boat with all the fixings. The salesman is still bragging about the whopper he reeled in.

"Maybe we should try another spot," J.D. says.

We could be fishing over Gorton's frozen fish sticks and J.D. still wouldn't get a nibble.

"Fish are like women," I say. "The harder you chase them, the less interested they are."

No one in the family could ever figure out what J.D. did for a living. I'm not sure Midge even knew. When you get past doctor, lawyer, Indian chief, our eyes glaze over.

Suddenly, my coffee starts splashing and the boat feels like it's going to capsize. I'm about to tell J.D. to settle down, when I hear a tinkle. There are different schools of thought concerning relieving oneself off the side of the boat while fishing. Regardless of your position, it's best not to rock the boat while a man's in the middle of the stream.

In the midst of all this, there's a squeal as J.D.'s reel spins like a Maytag. It scares him so bad he kicks his rod. It would have gone over the side if it hadn't snagged on his argyle socks. Apparently, the only thing the boat salesman didn't sell was outdoor clothing.

His hands shaking, J.D. grabs the line.

"Grab the rod!" I yell.

The fish glares up at us from the bottom of the boat. He is as old as dirt. There's a rusty hook in his mouth that's been there so long his skin has grown around it. And although his body is exhausted, there's still fight in his eyes.

"He's bigger than the one mounted at the bait shop," J.D. says, leaning over his trophy.

J.D. spent thirty-five years fighting his way up the corporate ladder. When he got to the top, they put a plaque in the lobby with his name on it.

The fish is as still as death, as if he knows what's about to come. One finger hooked through the gill, the other hand under the body, J.D. very gently lowers the fish back into the water. Floating on his side for a moment, his one eye stares up at J.D. Then the tail snaps like a whip and he's gone.

"Do you think he'll be O.K.?" J.D. asks, staring out at the lake.

I think he's just getting started.

Wiener Girls

Y OU HUNGRY?" SWEETIE ASKS.

I follow Sweetie's gaze to a hot-dog wagon, where a bronzed girl wearing a thong bikini and a smile is beckoning. Let's just say hot dogs are not the only thing she's steaming up. They call them "Wiener Girls" down here in Florida, and they're the cause of at least ninety percent of the rear-end collisions in the state.

Now, a lot of women probably wouldn't like their men buying foot-longs from a girl equipped with toasted buns, but it's my philosophy that a guy will never fly coach as long as he's got a first-class ticket.

Unfortunately, every so often, I have to take my philosophy out of my mouth and put it where I live.

"Look, but don't touch," I say, pushing him off the hood of the car.

Sweetie and I are propped on top of a rental car, backs against the windshield, waiting for a jet to take off in the dark. When I told Sweetie I wanted this to be a night I wouldn't forget, this wasn't exactly the liftoff I had in mind.

In Orlando, according to Sweetie, only the bourgeois watch the million-dollar fireworks extravaganza at the Magic Kingdom. The traveler-in-the-know is mingling with the locals at the end of the airport runway, waiting for a plane to start its decline a little too early and grind them all into pâté.

I'm sure the fact that it costs $39.50 *each* to get into Disney, while plane watching is basically a dime's worth of gas and two Puffs tissues to wipe the dust off the hood, has nothing to do with it.

Plane watching is the new *extreme* sport for the danger-seeking lawn chair crowd. As far as the eye can see, loners straddling motorcycles and sucking on cigarettes, moms and dads feeding sandwiches to their broods out of coolers, and kids with Jimi Hendrix grinding on the radio are lined up on either side of us. Kind of like a ValuJet tailgate party.

"The key to successful plane watching is alignment," Sweetie informs me, as he slides us into position. "O.K. Here she comes."

In an otherwise pitch-black sky, three lights, which might be stars if they weren't moving, slowly come into focus. As the lights get brighter, someone turns Jimi up and the heart beats faster. Finally, this huge metal bird the size of a small town in Alabama, only with a little less red around the rim, is all you can see. As it thunders down the part in your hair, it sucks the breath right out of you.

While the rest of my girlfriends are being wooed with boxes of Godiva and flashing rings that come with Ray-Bans to keep from blinding you, I'm a hood ornament on a '96 Buick.

"Well," Sweetie says, "what do you think?"

I think it's a night I'll never forget. When I am old, I will remember this moment and smile—assuming the Wiener Girl hasn't cut me down in the prime of life with food poisoning.

Of course, I'm not about to let Sweetie know this. Without mystery, a girl's just another pair of legs in control-top pantyhose.

"This is it?" I ask. "A hot dog and planes landing in the dark?"

Sweetie throws me a box of Raisinettes.

"Well, that's more like it," I say, ripping into the cellophane.

It seems to me a good relationship is a lot like watching planes land in the dark. You need proper alignment, a modicum of comfort, and if it doesn't suck the breath right out of you, what's the point?

The Blues

❧

It's Saturday night and Sweetie and I are sitting in a blues bar somewhere in Memphis. Being the only white people in the place, we look like a couple of butter beans in a pot of pintos.

"You playing tonight, Sweetie?" a man asks, two glasses held above his head and his body turned sideways as he squeezes by our table.

Sweetie gives his chin a little lift of acknowledgment. Cigarette hanging on his lip and eyes narrowed to slits, his fingers drum the barbecue sauce on our tablecloth. If the boy gets any cooler, I'm going to have to defrost him before I take him home.

While other kids dreamed of growing up to be president, Sweetie dreamed of becoming Ray Charles. Growing up a middle-class white boy with perfect vision was tough on him.

"Pearl wants to know if you're planning on playing tonight, Sweetie?" our waitress asks, setting a fresh glass on the table.

Sweetie tilts his head back and slowly exhales a white plume to the ceiling, a mere molecule in the carcinogenic cloud hanging over us.

Other than an occasional candle, the only light in the place is a fifteen-watt bulb aimed at the musicians. Sticking a finger in my glass, I feel for an ice cube to make sure I'm not drinking the ashtray.

Hearing a woman humming with the music behind me, I swivel around and squint into the abyss.

Underneath an iridescent pearl headpiece are eyes the color of amber. Moving like hot fudge, the woman pours herself into a chair at our table and crosses legs that are two feet longer than my entire body.

"How's it goin', white chocolate?" Pearl says, like she can taste the words.

"Can't complain," Sweetie responds.

Sweetie's voice has suddenly dropped two octaves lower than the one he walked in with. Somewhere between the front door and our table, he morphed into James Earl Jones.

Pearl and Sweetie dive into a discussion about music. It's muddy waters to me. My only experience with the blues is John Belushi and Dan Aykroyd in *The Blues Brothers.* And I'm thinking, two rich white guys from Canada may not be the best foundation to build one's understanding of an African-American art form which evolved from total despair.

Resting my chin in my hand, I slip into a glassy eyed, electric guitar induced daze. When I come to, Pearl has Sweetie by the hand and is guiding him to the piano. I can't get the boy to scoot over on the couch. For this woman, he corners like a Ferrari.

Sliding onto the piano bench, Sweetie takes one last drag before balancing his cigarette on the edge of the keyboard. Then Sweetie plays and the world stops to listen.

The music pours like warm honey. It starts at the top of the head and slowly works its way down. When you feel your bones start to melt, you're torn between weeping and the overwhelming urge to lick something. If this ain't the blues, the rabbit's a goner.

"What's wrong, baby girl?" a man at the table next to me asks. "Ain't you ever heard the blues before?"

The man has the blackest skin I have ever seen. When he closes his eyes, he disappears.

"I'll tell you a little secret that most white folks don't understand," he says, leaning close. "See, it's the blues that makes the music, not the music that makes the blues."

"You're a musician?" I ask.

"Periodontist," he says, handing me his card.

Hey, who better to explain the blues than the King of Pain?

Agnostics

ACCORDING TO SWEETIE, THERE ARE THREE types of men: straight, gay, and guys who dress nice but aren't gay. Sweetie considers this last group confused and calls them agnostics.

"So," Weston says, "apparently you haven't tried the new wrinkle-free cotton."

"Can't say that I have," Sweetie says, glaring at me across the table.

Sweetie and I are having dinner with a friend. Well, actually, Wes is *my* friend. Sweetie thinks of him more like a pest Orkin hasn't quite figured out how to eradicate.

Tonight, dinner is on Wes, or more likely his expense account, celebrating his having made partner at his firm. Normally, I feel a little guilty chowing down on a baked potato that costs more than a bucket of the Colonel's, but it's amazing how someone else picking up the tab quells the conscience.

"Wrinkle-free cotton changed my life," Weston continues, his pinkie stiffly held at a ninety-degree angle from his aperitif. "I haven't got a clue what to do with my Friday nights now."

Sweetie is about to suggest what he can do, when I rein him in with a stare.

"You know it causes impotence," Sweetie says nonchalantly.

"What?" Weston says.

"The stuff they put on the cotton," Sweetie says. "You got to figure anything that makes a wrinkle go limp is bound to wipe the smile off Mr. Happy."

"He's kidding, right?" Weston asks.

With Sweetie, it's hard to tell.

During times like these, I feel it's best to adopt the United Nations' peacekeeping position—observe, but do not engage in the conflict.

Nibbling on a breadstick, I check out the other diners. When these people sweat it's 24K. Another thing one can't help but notice is how Four Star restaurants encourage family values. At least a half a dozen men are cuddling in the corners with their nieces.

Two hours spent discussing laundry is starting to take its toll on Sweetie. When Wes starts his "silk versus cotton boxers" soliloquy, Sweetie lights a cigarette. You can always tell when Sweetie's irritated. One drag on his nicotine delivery device and that sucker's ash to the filter.

For dessert, Wes orders flaming Cherries Jubilee for the three of us. The waiter prepares it like a magician. The polished copper saucepan glitters in the candlelight and the ruby red pile of succulent cherries makes the mouth water.

A twist of the wrist, a wave of the hand, and *Voila!* we have twelve-foot flames shooting to the ceiling and cherry juice falling like rain.

Someone screams "FIRE!" and suddenly we're in Beirut. While our hysterical waiter dances around hurling flaming cherry bombs, women scream, and uncles, pushing and shoving, abandon their nieces, who can't quite hurdle chairs in stiletto heels.

Meanwhile, Weston has turned into a Roman candle. Molten Jubilee is blazing a trail down the front of his still extremely crisp shirt. Hands waving at his shoulders like fish fins, he huffs and puffs, trying to blow himself out before the cherry napalm comes to a puddle on his privates.

Through it all, Sweetie never bats an eye. Cigarette dangling out the corner of his mouth, he calmly tosses his dessert plate over the flaming pan and, grabbing my ice water (with lemon), hurls it on Wes.

"Apparently, you haven't tried the new flame-retardant cotton," Sweetie says.

"He's kidding, right?" Weston asks.

With Sweetie, it's hard to tell.

Ode to the Purple Sweatshirt

Y ESTERDAY A FRIEND CALLED TO TELL ME SHE
was breaking up with her longtime boyfriend.

"I just couldn't take it anymore," she said.

"It was the Dallas Cowboys T-shirt, wasn't it?" I said.

"Was it that obvious?"

"We all saw it coming," I said knowingly.

Rule number one: The more secure a guy gets in a relationship, the worse he dresses. Rule number two: There will
eventually come a day when one particular piece of clothing
will drive the woman totally and completely insane.

For me it was the purple sweatshirt.

The purple sweatshirt was a souvenir from our vacation
in Hawaii. I liked it at first. In fact, I bought it for him. And
for the first year I was pleased that he wore it. I would have
preferred he didn't wear it *every day*, but after all, it was kind
of a compliment.

Moving into the second year, he only took the purple
sweatshirt off for funerals and weddings, and I started getting
slightly annoyed.

At my cousin's suggestion, I tried "substitution." She's a
psychologist; she knows about these things.

I bought him other sweatshirts, very expensive, soft, over-sized sweatshirts, just the way he likes them. He shunned them with disdain.

Positive reinforcement followed. Whenever he didn't wear the purple sweatshirt, I lavished him with praise.

"Sweetheart, you're wearing a white shirt and tie. You're beautiful. You're irresistible. I don't think I can keep my hands off of you. You look like a Greek god. I spit on Andy Garcia. (*Spit. Spit.*) It's you, and only you I want."

When he pulled the purple sweatshirt over the white shirt and tie, I decided maybe it's a culture thing. You know, like maybe he doesn't have any.

By this time the sweatshirt is beginning to look a bit worn, and he has started coordinating the rest of his wardrobe to match. Translation: They have pulled miners out of collapsed mines who were better dressed.

Various multicolored stains adorn the front. The cuffs look like rats have been gnawing on them, and scientists are applying for grants to study the organisms living in the collar.

My cousin, the psychologist, suggests I "point out well-dressed men in the hopes he will emulate them." Translation: Make him jealous.

"My, isn't he an attractive and well-dressed man?" I comment as we walk through the mall.

"He's gay."

"Really?" I say, swiveling my head 180 degrees to follow the man down the hall.

"Yeah, gay."

"How do you know?" I ask.

"The shoes," he says, the "of course" left implied.

Shoes? You mean, they have gay shoe stores?

He rolls his eyes. "It's obvious. Look at his shoes. Like

new. Not a scuff. And," he adds, raising his eyebrows, "they're Italian."

A dead giveaway. How could I have missed it?

"So, let me get this straight," I say. "Only gay men wear very nice, expensive, polished shoes, and straight men wear..." I look down at his shoes. I'm not sure what style they are, but they look like he's been on a cattle drive.

"Right," he says with total assurance. "Straight men don't worry about how they dress."

This may also explain why, to add insult to injury, the purple sweatshirt is inside out.

"Wait a minute. You worried about how you dressed when I first met you," I counter.

He pauses on this, and silly me, I actually thought I had him.

"I was gay then," he says. "You turned me into a straight guy."

"You were dating the entire women's choir when I met you."

"Yes," he says, nostalgically, "but they weren't half the woman you are."

Nineteen ninety-seven will mark the sixth year of his, or maybe my, obsession with the purple sweatshirt. I dream of pouring acid on it, burning it, and stapling it to a railcar bound for Mexico.

Meanwhile, all across the world, women are fantasizing about the men who used to pick them up for dates, dressed like they were trying to impress them.

I wonder what men fantasize about. Could it be the size six we women used to be?

Nah.

Baby Pushers

To BREED OR NOT TO BREED, THAT IS THE question. Having children—it's a tough decision. On the one hand I picture myself all alone at the nursing home, gumming chocolate-covered cherries on Christmas Eve. On the other hand, I have vicariously experienced motherhood through my friends, and it ain't been all oatmeal cookies and Purity milk.

For the most part parenthood seems to follow the same path:

Phase one: "We're going to have a BA-BEE."

A Berlitz tape for speaking "Parent" must come with the home pregnancy kit. Parents-to-be never say "baby"; they say "BA-BEE," as though a choir of angels were singing the "Hallelujah Chorus" in the background.

Phase two: "The Child Is Born."

And what a little bundle of joy it is. Defying every known physical law, wonder-baby sleeps in fifteen-second intervals, produces twice as much waste as it consumes, and emits delightful little noises that dolphins can hear in the mid-Atlantic.

While Dad struts around the living room, bragging about "what a piece of cake" the fourteen hours of labor was,

Mom—strategically propped at a forty-five degree angle—
looks like someone just liposuctioned her soul out of her . . .
Well, you get the picture.

Phase three: "The Child Is Gifted!"

Strangely, every one of my friends has given birth to an
"advanced and gifted" child. How they know this when Kid
still can't hold his head up, I'm not sure. Maybe it's the way
he eats. Apparently, normal children chew and swallow.
Gifted kids let you fill up their mouths, and then stare at you
until the pabulum dries to a concrete-like consistency. You
have to wonder why we need schools.

Phase four: "The Titillating Twos."

For two hours you sit and listen to how brilliant, creative,
and musically inclined Kid is. Mom and Dad tell you this as
"young Einstein" runs around the room screaming at the top
of his lungs, pulling the hair out of your dog's ears, and col-
oring on the cabinets.

Mom wants to control him, honest she does, but it's just
so darned difficult to focus these days. And after two years of
fragmented marital relations, Dad is—oh, how shall we put
it—wound a little tight.

Phase five: "The Real Reason Thirteen Is Unlucky"

When Kid turns thirteen, Mom and Dad begin to fear he
might not be quite as bright as they originally thought. In
fact, they're thinking brain dead.

Most of Kid's conversations are on the level of a belliger-
ent talking parrot, an endless series of monosyllabic words re-
peated in a mindless manner. "Huh? Why? How come? You
know. Why? Huh?"

And "Gifted Child" is failing gym.

Phase six: "The A-Parent Error—or Omen IV."

When Kid turns sixteen, Mom and Dad begin to doubt
they are the biological parents of the demon living in their

kitchen. It is also around this time that Mom trades *Good Housekeeping* for *Cosmo*, and Dad starts every conversation with, "Don't get me wrong, I love my kid, but if I had it to do over. . . ."

Phase seven: "I Want to Be a Doctor . . . or a Bartender at the Hard Rock Cafe."

The dream of a scholastic scholarship having faded to a bleached bone-knuckle white, parents now foster the naive notion that Kid will "work his way through college—like we did." The only problem is, at todays tuition Kid would have to be a part-time neurological surgeon just to pay for his parking decal. Parents begin to "live lean."

Phase eight: "I Need a Little Time to Get it Together."

Translation: Kid drops out of college. Moves back home. Gets part-time job with Greenpeace.

This is as far as any of my friends have made it, and by golly, it sure makes me want to rush right out and get in the motherly way.

I suppose you're wondering where Sweetie stands on all this. After all, it does take two. Well, recently he told me he definitely, absolutely, positively did not want children.

I took this to mean he hasn't made up his mind either.

Beauty and the Bathing Suit

$\curlywedge$

SWEETIE," I SAY TO MY BELOVED, "I'VE BEEN thinking about getting my hair cut like Raquel Welch."

When he wrinkles his brow in thought, I assume he's trying to picture me with Raquel's elegant, yet playful style.

"Raquel Welch has hair?" he says.

We women don't have a clue. Most of us think beauty is located somewhere above the chin. But the fact is, Prince Charming didn't raise his eyes any higher than Cinderella's Peter Pan collar until the day he lifted the wedding veil to kiss her.

You thought that surprised look on your new hubby's face was the thrill of marriage? Honey, that boy was getting his first good look at you. Wake up and smell the perm.

Woman's first realization that man's definition of beauty has nothing to do with cheekbones and lustrous hair usually comes at the beach.

"Good golly, Miss Molly!" Sweetie gasps under his breath.

Tilting up my Ray-Bans, I catch a not too inconspicuous glimpse of a woman setting up camp in front of us.

Let's just say, I'm sure she has a great personality.

Meanwhile, Sweetie has turned into Jerry Lee Lewis. His feet are thumping the sand and his thumbs are drumming the arms of his lounge chair as he growls, "Goodness, gracious—GREAT BALLS OF FIRE!"

Now, I'm not the kind of woman who objects to her man checking out other women. I think it keeps a man frisky. On the other hand, even a good dog barks up the wrong tree every now and then.

"Sweetheart," I say, "perhaps we should get you out of the sun."

"You're just jealous," he says.

Ooooh . . . don't you just hate it when they do that!?

"Are you kidding?" I huff. "Lassie wouldn't lick that face!"

"Face??"

Based on the Love-of-My-Life's subtle response, I decide to reevaluate the lady in question.

When a woman sizes up the competition, it usually goes something like this: Hair, makeup, face, jewelry, clothes—then we check out her hair again. We almost never get around to the body unless we suspect she's wearing the new Wonder Girdle, which not only shapes, but also lifts like an air operated car jack. Truly one of the great innovations of our time.

Since the woman in question has no makeup, jewelry, or cheekbones, I pass right on to the clothes.

She's wearing three Day-Glo pink Post-it notes strung together with fishing line.

"Pink really doesn't go with her skin tone," I say.

"Sweetheart," he says, "perhaps we should get you out of the sun."

A recent scientific study determined that man's definition

of beauty is strictly biological, and is based on the woman's ability to bear and nurse his children.

A similar study determined woman's attraction to man is based on his ability to protect and provide for her and her offspring.

Translation: Men like big boobs. Women like big billfolds.

Cars Make the Man

I WAS BROUGHT UP TO BELIEVE THAT A GUY WHO didn't know the difference between a V-6 and a V-8 was probably running about a quart low on testosterone.

"If that boy doesn't keep a *Car and Driver* by his toilet," my dad used to say, "introduce him to your cousin, Maurice."

Fortunately, not only did Sweetie subscribe to *Car and Driver*, he used the Dewey Decimal System to catalogue the back issues. It was love at first flush.

One of the first things a girl discovers about a guy is, he spends a lot of time on car lots—not that he has any intention of buying a car. It's just something men do. Dogs mark their territory. Men sniff Corinthian leather.

You know a guy is getting serious about you when he takes you along for the Sunday afternoon "Parade of Car Lots." And there's no place a girl would rather be than spending her day stomping across molten pavement, with a guy ooohing and ahhhing because they've modified the blinkers on the '98 model.

Used to, I could actually tell one car from another. A Cadillac looked like a Cadillac, and a Honda looked like a sewing machine.

But nowadays everything's a blur. Jaguars have become

Fords, and a Chrysler is really a Mitsubishi. When I'm kicking GM tires I really get confused.

"Now, is this the GM that's made by Suzuki or Toyota?" I ask.

"Isuzu," my Sweetie huffs, flabbergasted by my ignorance.

With today's GM, along with the thirty-six-month warranty, you get a fortune cookie. Of course, none of this really matters since they all look like Honda Accords to me, except the Honda Accord, which looks like a Honda Civic.

When I was in college any single girl without a recent *Automotive Blue Book* was either too stupid to know better or too rich to care. I had a girlfriend who could tell you the make, model, and resale value from a second-story dorm room while watching *Dynasty*.

A guy's car denoted his marital status, his economic bracket, his self-image, and—if you were really good—his religious affiliation. A good Baptist drove a Chevy, and an agnostic usually owned a Volvo and a Saab. They never could seem to make up their minds.

If a guy drove a Jeep you knew he was the outdoor type. Nowadays a guy forks out thirty-five grand for a four-wheel drive so he can make it over the pile of mulch that fell out of his landscaper's truck.

Granted, it is nice not to have to put a quart of oil in every time you stop for gas. But I miss the days when cars had a personality and said something about the personality of the driver. Cars used to be exciting. Cars used to be sexy.

I remember the night my dad brought home a 1965 gold Mustang fastback. One at a time, he took each of us kids for a drive around the neighborhood. With lust in their hearts—and their dinner napkins still tucked in their collars—men came out of their houses to stare.

Maybe I'm wrong, but somehow I doubt kids jump up and down for a tour around the block in Dad's new Corolla—the Barry Manilow of cars.

Intellectually, I know cars are merely a form of transportation that moves a person from point A to point B. I know a car is not really an extension of a person's ego.

But the other day, while I was sitting at a stoplight, a black Porsche 911 growled to a stop next to me. I felt a flush run over my skin. With as much "nonchalant" as I could muster, I slowly turned, making eye contact with the driver.

It was my cousin, Maurice. He's dating a proctologist.

My Grave Concern

W HEN MOM COMES TO VISIT, THE FIRST PLACE she wants to go is the graveyard. It's usually an all-day affair. My family has almost as many skeletons below ground as in the closet.

"Oh, there's your great-uncle Harvey," Mom says, pulling Sis and me to a stop in front of a tilting tombstone. "You remember Uncle Harvey."

Uncle Harvey used to find great joy in putting his glass eye in the coleslaw at family reunions. No amount of therapy could get me to eat coleslaw now.

Mom, never having seen much distinction between the living and the dead, is dressed like she's having tea with the queen. My little sister is going through her "Madonna meets the Cherokee" phase. And I'm in my usual "fashion follows function." If I had on a hard hat, we'd look like a female version of The Village People.

Even if Mom owned a pair of sensible shoes, I doubt she'd wear them. On this particular day she's teetering on two-inch red spikes. Every time she takes a step, her heels drive into the ground like tent stakes. Then, with the momentum of pulling her foot free, her knee pops up to her waist. She looks like a cross between a Rockette and a Tennessee Walking Horse.

With Sis at one elbow and me at the other, Mom aerates the memorial lawn.

"Dear Aunt Molly," Mom says. "The finest teacher in the county."

Dear Aunt Molly used to entertain us by dressing up in a grass skirt and bra, and doing the hula while reciting risqué limericks.

When we get to an unusually well-kept grave, Mom seems to draw a blank.

"Oh, Cousin Claudia," she finally says, reading the marker.

It doesn't ring a bell for me. I look over at Sis. She's yawning.

"Oh, you remember, Claudia," Mom says. "She was a very good housekeeper."

Well, that narrows it down.

Other than her victory over dust, Claudia must have been as boring as toast. Mom pulls out a compact and checks her teeth for lipstick. Sis lights a cigarette, and I chew off a hangnail. After a respectable amount of time, we move on.

Apparently, this party isn't moving fast enough to suit Mom. Pulling free, she wobbles off on tiptoe while Sis and I lean against a tree to enjoy the ambiance.

Our family graveyard is what a graveyard should be, old and spooky.

Nowadays, they plant you like corn, in perfectly straight rows with perfectly uniform markers flat on the ground, so they don't have to weed-eat. I would die. I want my eternal resting place to be wild and unpredictable, with my headstone just slightly off center and facing in whatever direction I choose. In other words, I want death to resemble life as much as possible.

To end up like cousin Claudia makes me shudder. When my relatives stand in front of my grave, I want them to have something to talk about.

"If I turn into a boring person," I say, "I want you to let me know."

Slowly, Sis exhales a chain of white rings into my face.

"Consider yourself notified," she says.

It is a brief moment of sisterly love. Mom has mired at Great Aunt Hattie's and we have to go dig her out.

Sweetie's Workout

SWEETIE'S IDEA OF A GOOD CARDIOVASCULAR workout is slipping Cindy Crawford's exercise video into the VCR, lighting a cigarette, and breathing hard for thirty minutes.

"You know she was a math major," I say, watching Cindy pump, pout, and undulate in various modes of undress. "I'm sure that comes in handy counting all those repetitions."

"Don't distract me," Sweetie puffs. "I'm trying to keep my heart rate up."

I leave Sweetie—pupils bouncing to Cindy's mole like he's watching a sing-along—to his pursuit of physical excellence.

"Where's Sweetie?" Philo asks, waist deep in my refrigerator.

"Working out," I say.

"Ahhh . . . Cindy," he sighs, before tossing a meatball in the air and catching it in his teeth.

"Other than the size of their . . . egos, guys are all pretty much the same, aren't they?"

"Man wallows in the delusion that he's a one-of-a-kind, unique creation," Philo says. "Fact is, we're as common as Handiwipes at a nursery school."

Philo was working on his Ph.D. in philosophy when he found his true calling—professional barbecue competitions. Now, he travels the country with a giant stainless-steel barbecue pit shaped like a pig, spreading hog to the masses.

In my never-ending quest for self-improvement, and to be "all that I can be" for my Sweetie, I think it's important to evaluate what Cindy can give him that I can't—other than physical perfection and money beyond comprehension.

"What's the deal with men and models?" I ponder, licking peanut butter off a spoon. (It's reduced fat, so it takes twice as much to achieve a solace high.)

"It's a Zen thing," Philo says.

I have to admit models have taken the concept "No-Mind" to a whole new level.

"When I was in Nam," Philo continues, stroking his beard nostalgically, "one of the guys in my unit became obsessed with a girl who was a bra model in the Sears-Roebuck catalog. It took him over a year, but he finally got Sears to give him the name of her modeling agency. Then he convinced the modeling agency to forward his letters to her. Eventually, he convinced her to meet him while he was on leave in Hawaii."

If the army brass had had that kind of persistence, they'd be eating Kentucky Fried Chicken in Hanoi right now.

"How romantic," I say. "What happened?"

"She turned out to be a real airhead," Philo says, "but she had legs from here to Honolulu."

Sweetie stumbles into the kitchen with a towel around his neck, squirting water into his mouth from a squeeze bottle.

"How was your workout?" Philo asks.

"Cindy just doesn't push me to the level she used to," Sweetie shrugs.

"I hear Kathy Ireland has a new video out," Philo says.

"Now there's a girl who can get the heart pumping," says Sweetie.

Every so often, I know exactly how Jane Goodall, the anthropologist, must have felt when that gorilla let her pick through his fur for lice. I just haven't figured out yet if I'm studying the gorilla or the lice.

College: The Worst Years of Your Life

~

SOME ANIMALS EAT THEIR YOUNG. WITH HU-
mans, it's the other way around.

"I'll have a cup of hot water," Annie says to the waitress.
"You don't charge for hot water, do you?"

Annie just shipped her kid off to college, and was a little
surprised to find that his college fund barely covered the
freight on his CD's.

"I've had the cable disconnected, the garbage pick-up dis-
continued, and stopped all the magazines," Annie says, as she
dumps the bowl of Equal into her purse. "Anybody know
how many times a week you can give blood?"

Maxine whips out her donor card and passes it over.

Baby ducks sink or swim. Baby birds fly or fall. But baby
humans cling to your checkbook until the nursing home
pries their little fingers off.

"Has he decided on a major?" I ask, picking through
my salad.

"Theater," Annie says, dropping the napkin holder into
her purse next to the toilet paper.

"Good grief!" Rosie says. "Why doesn't he just smash a
pillow over your face and get it over with?"

Nothing like hocking the house so your kid can do dinner theater in Jersey.

"Oh, he'll change majors before it's all over," Maxine says. "In fact, he'll change majors half a dozen times."

Maxine pours a little cream in her coffee.

"Then, of course, he'll change schools—losing half his credits—because his girlfriend said his eyes clash with the school colors."

Maxine's knuckles are starting to get a little white, and hairline cracks are forming on the coffee cup she's gripping.

"Then, there's the moving expenses, the apartment deposit, the electric deposit, the phone deposit, the cost of fumigation when his iguana dies in the heating ducts. . . ."

By this time, people around us are starting to stare. The veins in Maxine's temples are throbbing like hamster hearts, and the wine glasses hanging over the bar are starting to rattle.

"Then, one month before graduation—after he's sucked you clean as a lobster claw—he calls to tell you he isn't sure he wants to spend the rest of his life as a cardiologist, has dropped out of school, and is working as a towel boy at a Holiday Inn pool!"

The couple at the table next to us is staring at Maxine like she has a baby Reebok dangling out of her mouth.

"Of course," Maxine says, eyes narrowed, "I wouldn't trade him for the world."

"Rosalyn is majoring in psychology at Columbia, you know," Rosie says, wrapping the string around her tea bag to squeeze it dry. "Now, when she calls to blame me for all her problems, she cites case studies and uses the clinical terms for my inadequacies."

"Kind of makes you wish you'd drowned that puppy, doesn't it?" Maxine says, crunching on a crouton.

"Tell me. Do I strike you as an 'anal retentive dominatrix'?" Rosie asks.

"Isn't 'dominatrix' like a sexual thing?" Annie asks, frowning.

We all stare at Rosie.

"Your kid's an idiot," Maxine huffs. "You don't have a sexual bone in your body."

"Thank you, Maxine," Rosie says.

Dr. V.

MY LEGS MAY LOOK LIKE PANTYHOSE STUFFED with cottage cheese, but I have great teeth. I credit my pearly whites to two things: first, having my mouth regularly scrubbed with various abrasive cleansers as a child, and second, my dentist, Dr. V.

Not to take anything away from Mom and her futile efforts to turn me into a lady, but when it comes to teeth, Dr. V. is the Rolls-Royce of dentists. And he's about in the same price range.

But I figure you get what you pay for. And what I'm paying for is the absolute certainty that when Dr. V. lets his fingers do the walking around my uvula, he knows exactly where he's going, won't be tracking in any unwanted reminders of previous exhibitions, and that my mouth will be so numb you could string my lips with Christmas lights and I wouldn't know it.

I do not like pain. I don't even like the potential of pain. I am therefore extremely apprehensive when it comes to dentists. When someone says to me, "This won't hurt a bit" then proceeds to jam a two-inch needle in my jaw, I reason, this person and I do not share the same definition of pain.

You can imagine then, how I felt when Dr. V. broke the news I needed gum surgery.

"Gum surgery?"

"It's a simple procedure," Dr. V. assured me. "We're going to slice away the top half of your gums, peel them down to expose the upper tooth root, then using a very sharp—"

When I came to I was already strapped onto the operating chair.

I believe the moment apprehension graduated to hysteria came when I got a glimpse of the latest in dental apparel. Dr. V. and his assistant were wearing full rubber suits, bubble helmets with face shields, steel belted rubber gloves, and double-air tanks.

I began to suspect this operation resulted in considerable bloodshed, which naturally led me to wonder who—or exactly what—had been in the operating chair before me, and was I sitting on it.

"This is going to hurt a little," Dr. V. said, as he vacuum-locked the door, "but you'll thank me when it's over."

Yeah, right. And Sonny Bono will someday be president.

Dr. V.'s assistant, whom I have always felt enjoyed her job just a tad too much, leaned over me, smiling.

"Now, if you need to scream," she said, "you go right ahead."

"Wait! Wait," I yelled, hooking Dr. V. with the one finger I could still move freely. "Let's just suppose I opted against this gum surgery. What are we looking at here?"

"Your jaw would drop, your teeth would fall out, and within six months you'd look like Gabby Hayes," Dr. V. said matter-of-factly.

"I could live with that," I assured him.

The nurse snapped a little plastic cup over my nose and told me to count backward from one hundred. Shortly before

I got to ninety-nine I was no longer in this world. Dr. V. could have deboned me and I wouldn't have cared.

I woke up feeling like someone had stretched my lips over a basketball, shoved my mouth in a Cuisinart, and then stuffed it with bubble wrap.

"Now, that wasn't so bad, was it?" Dr. V. asked.

"Aaar ooo azee?!!" I mumbled.

Which loosely translated means, "Do they teach you guys this stuff, or is a total lack of reality a prerequisite for dental school?"

"Don't eat any solids for a while," Dr. V. continued, "and expect to lose a little weight."

My ears perked. Did the man say "LOSE WEIGHT?!"

"Oww ooo ann ieee ooo isss ainnn?!" I garbled.

Which loosely translated means, "Exactly how many times a year can I get this done?"

Hey, a girl can't care too much about dental hygiene.

Pavarotti's Salami

◞∽◟

I T'S GOOD TUH KNOW THERE ARE STILL A FEW decent people left in this world," the woman says, as she picks something out of her hair, counts the legs, then flicks it in my direction.

The woman and I are standing on the side of the road watching Sweetie inspect her flat tire, or rather what's left of it. A Brillo pad has less steel showing.

"I had this fleetin' suspicion somethin' weren't quite right," she says, "when I seen them little bits a tire a bouncin' off the windshield of my Chevy."

Riding on the rim for ten miles must have been a little too subtle for her.

I'm sure her son would help Sweetie with the tire, but at the moment he's preoccupied with playing tic-tac-toe on his arm with a switchblade.

Looking up from his art work, Blade Boy sticks his tongue out at me and vibrates it like a hummingbird's wing.

"Stick that tongue back in yer mouth, boy, 'fore I bite it off!" Ma says. "I swear that child would flirt with a sow."

Somehow, I suspect this is not as far from the truth as one might hope, and I'm wondering where exactly that puts me on the food chain.

"Let's take a look at your spare," Sweetie says, standing up and dusting off his hands.

Creaking open the trunk lid, which is being held down with duct tape, Ma dives in head first, and proceeds to do a little housekeeping.

"We been sittin' here fer hours," she says, tossing beer cans, oil cans, and empty cigarette cartons over her shoulder onto the lawn next to where her car rolled to a stop.

Why the person inside the house, now peeking through the living room curtains, didn't rush to her assistance, remains a mystery.

When Ma finally unearths the spare, she slaps the fender and yells, "Key-yawn-tee! Git yerself out here!"

Slowly, the car door opens and a pair of long olive-skinned legs slides into view. As the rest of her six-foot frame emerges, traffic comes to a screeching halt. Wearing cutoffs worn to the thickness of cheesecloth and filling out a torn T-shirt in a way the rest of us can only dream of, Chianti unfolds herself from the car like a swan stretching its wings.

Tossing her long black hair, Chianti reaches into the trunk with one hand and picks up the tire like she's lifting a Krispy Kreme doughnut out of the box.

Sweetie, his communication skills reduced to sign language, points, and Chianti, barefooted, carries the tire around the car to where Blade Boy is stabbing the ground like a caveman.

"Her daddy wuz a *BIG* boy," Ma says, as we watch Chianti jack up the car. "He had a two-hour layover at the airport where I wuz handlin' baggage, and I guess you could say we shared more than a bottle of veee-no. He's a famous I-tal-ian opry singer, you know."

"Pavarotti!??" I say.

"Didn't ketch the name," Ma says, "but I shore loved that big salami."

Breaking the nuts loose, Chianti spins them off like a Black and Decker.

"Sing sumthin' off a' them records yer daddy left," Ma says.

Standing up, Chianti gazes at heaven as though she can see something the rest of us mortals can't. Then taking a deep breath, she parts lips the color of crushed grapes and sings.

Like an angel pouring out her soul, her perfect voice, in perfect Italian, pierces the air. The thought of this heavenly creature trapped with Ma and the Blade Boy brings tears to my eyes.

When she is finished, Chianti bows her head and sighs. Then, slowly opening her dark, soulful eyes, she looks down at Sweetie, sticks her tongue out, and vibrates it like a hummingbird's wing.

Elope

WHEN HER ONLY DAUGHTER ELOPED WITH AN unemployed French bartender, we had to hold Helen's head between her knees for a good forty-five minutes.

"How can you be an unemployed bartender in France?" Maxine asks, as she aims Helen's face down into a clean garbage can. "Those people drink like fish."

"Let's try and look at the bright side, shall we," Rosie says.

When we can't come up with a bright side, we do the next best thing—we talk about Maxine's kids. A ten-minute update on Maxine's brood would make Al Capone's mother proud.

The night the newlyweds are to arrive, more than two hundred of our closest friends gather in Helen's backyard, celebrants on the left, mourners on the right, and freeloaders equally dispersed.

Maxine rented a white tent the size of Barnum and Bailey's Big Top, and strings of white paper lanterns stretch from tree to tree like the landing strip at the Atlanta airport. Maxine is of the school that, the greater the humiliation, the more ostentatious the party.

While the guys straighten each other's chef's hats at the barbecue and Rosie barks orders in the kitchen, Maxine and I prop up Helen.

"I can't believe this is happening," Helen mutters, as we watch the guests buzz through the appetizers like locusts.

It is one of life's little myths that labor pains end at childbirth.

When the newlyweds are late, Rosie decides to start dinner without them. A mouth full of food won't stop gossip, but at least it muffles it. And so, the guests are up to their elbows in ribs when Helen's daughter, Doll, finally shows up.

Doll's a good kid, which is the cruel irony of this situation. If she weren't a good kid, she probably wouldn't be in this predicament. She also comes by her nickname honestly. Doll is so beautiful, it hurts to take your eyes off of her.

When Doll's new husband takes his place beside her, the unified gasps of two hundred people almost suck the Japanese lanterns off the trees. Whatever worries we had about this marriage made in France are quickly replaced by serious concerns as to exactly when this boy's ancestors first crawled onto dry land.

His eyes blink laboriously slow, like the lids have a little difficulty making it over the huge bulbous orbs, and his tongue, which appears to have a sticky quality to it, darts in and out between lips that stretch from ear-to-ear.

But the question on everyone's mind is, "Do you suppose that's the way they wear their hair in France, or is his head really pointed?"

He definitely has an amphibious air to him.

The crowd is speechless. Doll could have married any man she wanted, and we're all having a little trouble coupling her with Ker-meeet, the French frog man.

"Oh, Mom!" Doll exclaims, dragging her new husband in front of Helen. "Isn't he wonderful?"

Helen would throw herself in front of a train for Doll.

She would sleep on a bed of nails, and give Doll all her major organs. But how does a mother save her child from love?

"I need a drink," Helen says.

"Oui," her new son-in-law nods, and instinctively hops off toward the bar.

No one understands better than the French that some things are easier to swallow when they're covered in a little sauce.

Mrs. Snake at Mother's Hog Hut

W HEN IT COMES TO SAFETY IN THE WORKPLACE, there's one danger they never warn you about—getting pulverized by a coworker's spouse.

"You know how I'm always talkin' 'bout my old lady?" Snake says, as we're walking out to the parking lot.

"Yeah," I say, digging through my purse for keys.

"Well," he says, his eyes darting around, "she kinda wants to meet you."

"O.K." I shrug. "Tell her to give me a call."

"Well, see, she kinda wants to meet you, like . . . NOW," he says, kick-starting his Harley.

As Snake roars off into the horizon, a form slowly materializes in his exhaust—black leather miniskirt, leather drawstring halter stretched to capacity, skull earrings, and a tattoo of a knife dripping blood in the center of her cleavage.

Where does this woman shop? The Angel of Death Boutique?

"Mrs. Snake?" I say, thinking "Snake's Old Lady" might be a bit too familiar under the circumstances. "I've heard so much about you."

"Yeah?" she says. "Well, I been hearin' *too* much about you."

"What do you say we discuss this over coffee?"

I figure, if I'm about to meet my maker, I might as well be alert.

Apparently, Mother, proprietor of Mother's Hog Hut, doesn't get many requests for latté with skim milk.

"We got beer, beer, and . . . well, whadayaknow . . ." she says, rolling a toothpick from one side of her mouth to the other, ". . . beer."

I realize beer is an ancient and respected beverage in many cultures, but quite frankly, I'd just as soon drink spit. While Mother and Mrs. Snake aren't looking, I pour my brew on the floor. I assure you, no one will ever notice.

"Look," I finally say, "there's absolutely nothing going on between your husband and me."

Mrs. Snake rolls her head in my direction. "Yeah, well, that goes without sayin'. Your equipment ain't big enough for the job."

I feel fairly certain she's not referring to the size of my heart.

"Here's the deal," she says. "Last night my old man read the paper."

I roll this revelation over in my mind but, for the life of me, I can't quite make the connection between journalism and my being reduced to dust by the Terminator Wife.

"Every night we . . . *you know*. But last night, he like, READS THE PAPER."

"EVERY NIGHT?!" I say.

"Honey, face it. Chicks like you are sugar in a guy's gas tank. You talk to them 'bout stuff. Stuff leads to thinkin'. Thinkin' leads to NUTHIN'! You might as well take a guy to the vet and get him snipped."

"I never really thought about it like that."

"Hey," Mrs. Snake shrugs, "some of us have wheels. Some of us have to hitchhike."

The rest of the afternoon Mrs. Snake continues to en-lighten me, along with showing me how to shoot a bank shot in the corner pocket.

And Mother keeps them coming. As fast as I can pour them on the floor, Mother pours them in the mug. When there isn't a dry spot left on the floor, I figure it's probably time to go home.

"What do you say we do this again sometime?" I say, as Mrs. Snake climbs on her Harley Sportster.

"I don't think so," she says. "I don't hang with chicks who don't drive domestic."

She puts her bike in gear, then looks back at me.

"I will say this for you, though. You sure can hold your booze."

Golf

. . . AND ON THE EIGHTH DAY, GOD CREATED the fairway.

Mr. G. and I are standing on the eighteenth green at the country club. A black cloud has been following us all day, and the sky is pretty nasty, too.

"I always like to play a little golf before I do business," Mr. G. says, studying his grip. "You learn a lot about people by the way they handle a putter."

This being the case, Mr. G.'s a very patriotic man. His face is red, his knuckles are white, and the head of his Ping putter is starting to turn blue. Combine this with pea-green knickers and pumpkin pom-pom club covers, and you've got a guy who looks like a salad bar that's starting to go bad.

While I hold the flag, Mr. G., praying over his putter, tries to become "one" with the ball. He's already "one" with the hole, and I suspect has been all his life.

"She'll curve to the right," I say.

"What makes you think so?" he asks, not turning around.

Oh, I don't know. Could it be because we're leaning like the Tower of Pisa, and the green is so fast my marker is sliding toward the hole.

"Just a hunch," I say.

"A hunch won't buy my lunch, little lady," he says.

He should know. This man hasn't picked up a tab in two decades. He might as well be holding a sign that says, "Will do business for food."

Repositioning his grip, Mr. G. wiggles his derriere, and for five minutes paws the green like a cat in a litter box. After a dozen tease shots, he finally strokes the ball, sending her straight to the right. The ball does a perfect crescent, misses the hole by a yard, drops down the bank, and digs into the sand like a clam trying to make a getaway.

"Wedge!" he snaps.

Jogging back to the cart, I grab his wedge, sprint around the hole, and rendezvous for D-Day on the beach.

"Can't see the hole," Mr. G. says, tightening his gloves. "You'll have to go hold the flag."

Like this is really going to make a difference. God couldn't make this shot.

Looking for toe holds, I scale Hamburger Hill and raise the flag.

I'm still flossing with Bermuda grass when the ball comes arching over the bank and lands next to my foot like a homing pigeon. This is a phenomenal shot, especially since the wedge is still lying on the sand where I left it. It gives the term "pitching wedge" a whole new meaning.

"So, little lady," he says, taking his putter from me, "you're hoping to do a little business."

Actually, I'm hoping to do a lot of business. Do I strike you as the sort of person who'd suck up for pocket change?

"Well, I've been in this business since before you were born . . ."

God bless alpha hydroxy.

". . . and I'm wondering exactly what you think you can tell me that I don't know."

"The truth is, sir," I say, "next to you, I'm green as bent grass."

"Spreading it a little thick, aren't we, little lady?" he says, tapping his ball straight into the hole with a final plunk. "But, I suppose we could discuss this further over another nine holes."

"I've got the money, if you've got the time, sir," I say.

The difference between an amateur and a professional is, the professional keeps on stroking, even when he's choking.

Gift Giving

SWEETIE'S CHOICES IN GIFTS TEND TOWARD THE avant-garde (which is French for tasteless and bizarre).

"What's that?" I ask.

"It's Mom's gift," Sweetie says, throwing a box with a picture of a cow on the front into our basket.

" 'Genuine Cowpie'," I say, reading the label.

"It's a chocolate pie shaped like . . . ."

"I don't think so," I say, handing it back.

"But it's 'udderly delicious'," Sweetie says.

Last year, Sweetie gave his mother a commode plunger with a Pez dispenser built into the handle.

Then there was the year he dashed into a coin shop five minutes before closing. Nothing says "I love you" like a couple of Susan B. Anthony coins wrapped in a brown paper bag.

If Ripley's Believe It or Not ever opens an outlet mall, Sweetie will be first in line.

As soon as Mom unwraps her Gift of the Weird, every eye in the house always rolls my way. I ask you, am I my Sweetie's keeper?

But this year, I am not going to suffer through another humiliating gift opening. I've taken charge of Sweetie's mother's gift, and after eleven months of extensive research, I know exactly what she wants.

There, glittering in the storefront window, like a star in the East, is the perfect gift—a delicate cut-glass crystal nativity scene on a beveled oval mirror.

"She's going to love it," I say, bending over the glass case.

"Austrian leaded crystal," the salesman says, carefully lifting a Wise Man from the case and holding its twinkling facets to the light.

"I'll take it," I say, whipping out the plastic.

"An heirloom," the salesman says, sticking one of those mini telescopes in his eye to study the clarity. "Signed by the artist . . ."

"Yeah, yeah," I say. "Wrap her up."

"Perhaps Madam would be interested in the . . . detailing," he says, flipping over the price tag.

After I return from my near-death experience, I regroup.

"I don't suppose you have the same thing in like . . . jelly-jar glass?" I say.

Two cities, three malls, and twenty-nine stores later . . . .

"What's it made of?" I sigh, staring at the dusty display.

Snapping her gum, the salesgirl picks up a Wise Man and bangs him on the countertop.

"Could be glass," she says, listening to the dull clunk.

It is, of course, the last one, and the box is long gone. With the help of a little spit, I scrub off the MADE IN TAIWAN stickers, and drop the little figurines into my basket. Making my way to the checkout, the figurines roll and clink against each other like Coke bottles.

I finally get to the register, and as the checkout girl is dropping Joseph head first into a Certs box, I suddenly panic.

"Wait..." I say, picking up the tiny manger, "where's Jesus???!!!"

"Why, he's all around us, dear," the lady behind me says.

"Don't anybody move!" I shout.

Five people throw their arms in the air and someone tosses me their wallet.

Dropping onto all fours, I buff the linoleum as I retrace my path through the store, in search of baby Jesus. I might as well be looking for three wise men and a virgin.

"You'll see," Sweetie says, slapping a used bow on top of the box. "Mom's gonna love it."

Oh yeah, exactly what she's always wanted, The Gift of the Cowpie.

Joe's Boy

"WHAT HAVE I DONE?" JOE ASKS.

Apparently, marrying a woman less than half your age causes amnesia.

"Where was my brain?" Joe groans.

Someone hand the man a compass.

Sweetie, Joe, and I—feet propped up and ice clinking in the glasses—are kicked back on the deck watching the sun set. Joey Jr., the redheaded fruit of Joe's poor sense of direction, is sitting in his little plastic traveler, purring like a kitten.

Being the first child of Joe's child bride, J.J. is wrapped, strapped, and bound like King Tut. The only thing he can move is his tongue.

"If you don't loosen the kid up," Sweetie says, "I'm going to light him up and smoke him."

Sweetie is a tad bit irritable. He's in the first stages of quitting smoking—he's thinking about it.

Bending down, Joe gropes and fumbles with J.J.'s swaddling, until finally the kid can kick his little legs and wave his arms. The way he's fixating on his fingers, I have no doubt it's the first time he's seen them.

"The day he starts school," Joe says, rubbing his temples, "I'll be fifty-one."

About this time, Joe's new bride jogs past.

"Hi, baby!" she yells. "Just three more miles!"

Joe throws up his arm to wave and pulls a muscle.

"Joe," Sweetie says, his head following Lolita down the road, "you're a dead man."

". . . the day he gets his driver's license," Joe mutters, "I'll be sixty-one . . ."

Joe is still reviewing the periodic chart of his life when Lolita finishes her run and I take her into the house with me to fix that crème de la crème of appetizers—salsa and chips.

"You want to grab a shower?" I ask.

"Nah," she says, gulping down her third glass of water. "Joe likes me sweaty."

Wide-eyed, Lolita wanders around my kitchen like she's on a field trip at the Smithsonian.

"What's this?" she asks.

"It's a can opener," I say.

"So . . . like . . . is it solar?" she asks.

"No . . . like . . . it's manual," I say, opening the can of tomatoes.

"Whoa!" she says. "How environmental."

While I slice, dice, and mince, Lolita looks on like an intern observing her first bypass.

"You know," she says, "I bet you could teach me a lot of stuff."

I shrug modestly. It's not all bad having a few years under your belt, as long as they've been sucked, tucked, or lifted.

"So, like, I'm really worried," she says, digging her Air Nike into the rug. "Ever since J.J. was born, Joe and me aren't like we used to be."

"Joe's just going through postpartum," I say. "He'll get over it."

"It's like now that I'm a mother, he treats me *totally* different," she says.

"It's not uncommon for the libido to diminish following an increase in responsibility." Lolita is staring at me like someone just pulled the chip out of her main frame. "Libido," I say. "You know . . . his *desire*."

"Oh!" she says. "Well, his la-beat-O hasn't lost a beat. The problem is, he expects me to wait on him hand and foot!"

Forehead furled, Lolita looks at me in total despair.

"It's like now, I've got *two* babies!"

Like . . . welcome to womanhood.

Jump

SOMETIMES A GIRL GETS RESTLESS. SHE KNOWS if she doesn't do something quick they'll find her one day, OD'ed on Little Debbie snack cakes, with a bad home perm.

"I've decided to jump out of a plane," I say.

"Are you kidding?" Sweetie says. "You can't look down wearing two-inch heels."

"Yeah, so what's your point?"

Sweetie looks pensive, no doubt terrified by the prospect of losing me.

"Does your life insurance cover jumping out of planes?" he asks.

"Yeah," I say.

"Hey," he shrugs, "go for it!"

So early Saturday morning, while Sweetie is window shopping for BMWs, I drive toward my destiny, Sky Dive Paris, in Paris, Tennessee.

Basically, there are two ways to jump out of a plane, solo and tandem. From a layman's point of view, the difference is when you solo, you smash into the ground at 120 mph. When you tandem, you smash into the ground at 120 mph, then the 215-pound guy you're strapped to lands on top of you.

I opt for tandem. This means my instructor will be strapped to my back, and the parachute will be strapped to his. Think mating turtles.

"How much do you weigh?" Johnny, the owner of the flight school, asks as he fills out a form on a clipboard.

"Like, is this really critical information?" I ask.

"If we overload the plane it can't take off," he says.

I roll this piece of information over in my mind.

"One ten," I say.

He looks up from his clipboard and snickers.

About fifteen minutes before we take off, Johnny gets a call from another airport. One of his friends has tried out an illegal parachute. It didn't quite open in time and he broke his back.

"They're medi-vacing him to the hospital," he solemnly tells the crowd.

A silence falls over the room. Heads drop, eyes grow moist.

"Well," Johnny says, "LET'S DO IT!"

Young and alive, we sprint across the field to the waiting plane. (Actually, with the harness cutting into my crotch, it's more of a *Hunchback of Notre Dame* waddle, but I get there just the same.) There aren't any seats for the jumpers, so we throw ourselves on the floor behind the pilot.

Now, a lot of women would probably get a thrill out of being trapped in a confined space with a pile of guys in zip-up clothing. Of course this never crosses my mind.

It takes about twenty minutes to get to 10,500 feet. The guys are pumped, muscles flexing, nostrils flaring.

I had planned to spend the last few minutes of my life in meditative reflection. Unfortunately, I have this little problem. I always fall asleep in extreme stress, political speeches, and moving vehicles. In less than three minutes, I'm out like a light.

I wake up to find four guys staring at me. Inconspicuously, I check my chin for drool.

"It's her first jump," Johnny shouts over the engine.

The guys look at me in awe.

"It takes a 'real' guy to sleep before his first jump," a guy yells in my ear.

And it takes a "real" guy not to pee on herself.

Then it's time. Shouting war whoops and various other testosterone induced noises, one by one the guys throw themselves out the open door into the clouds.

I'm the last to go. Johnny nods. I kneel by the door and he snaps our harnesses together. We step outside the plane onto the wing. The air is cold, and the ground, two miles down, looks like a patchwork quilt. Johnny gives me the thumbs up. I lift my feet and arch my head back over his shoulder. He steps off the wing. And we fall.

There's a line in the opera *Tosca* that roughly translated goes, "Why is it I never truly loved life, until this moment before death?"

Of course, this came to me in retrospect. During the fall, I mainly wondered how I was going to unhook the corners of my mouth from my ears.

Kill Da Wabbit

THE CAT AND I ARE HIKING ALONG THE OLD logging road that runs through our property. The weather forecaster is calling for snow, so of course there isn't a cloud in the sky. Apparently, the U.S. Weather Service lacks one sophisticated piece of weather equipment—a window.

No one believes I have a hiking cat, but the fact is, this cat thinks he's a dog. It's Sweetie's fault. He started training him when he was a kitten. Now, Cat comes when you whistle, meows at the moon, and bites the UPS man.

In less civilized times, I might have had the urge to nibble on the tanned and extremely fit UPS man myself, but Sweetie has me trained, too. Basically, the cat and I have both been fixed.

We've been huffing and puffing along for about an hour, when suddenly Cat stops, lifts one paw, and points like a Brittany spaniel. Up ahead, a guy wearing a Day-Glo orange Elmer Fudd hat is hunched over, trying to tiptoe through the woods. It's never a good idea to disturb a hunter, but judging by the icicles hanging off his gun, I suspect Elmer is in need of a little assistance.

"Hey," I say.

"AAAAGH!" Elmer screams, twirling around in a panic and shaking his rifle at me.

It is times like these when you understand the value of a well-funded national defense program.

"Who are you?!" Elmer demands.

"I'm the person who tacked up that NO TRESPASSING sign you just passed," I say.

Once Elmer determines we're not going to make him drop on all fours and squeal like a pig, he just about jumps into my arms.

"How long have you been lost?" I ask.

"What day is it?" he asks.

Judging by the way Cat is wrapped around his new boots, Elmer went a little heavy on the deer musk.

"You don't strike me as the hunter type," I say, as I lead him back to the road.

"It's m-m-my boss," Elmer chatters, as he trips and stumbles along beside me. "He says hunting helps develop the k-k-killer instinct."

"You in the hit man training program?" I ask.

"Lawyer," Elmer says.

Same difference.

We're just about at my neighbor's property line when we see a white tail flash, and before I can stop him, Elmer throws the gun to his shoulder and fires.

I would have guessed Elmer couldn't hit a parked Boeing 747 if someone was holding the gun for him, but the animal goes stiff, teeters back and forth, then drops like a bowling pin.

"It's kind of small," Elmer says, as we stand over his kill.

"Actually," I say, "it's pretty big for a goat."

Evidently, Elmer's hunter safety class didn't stress the fact that deer don't wear bells around their necks.

Elmer drops onto a stump, and I'm assuming he's depressed about the legal ramifications of shooting my neighbor's goat, until I see the tear rolling down his frozen face.

As I'm pondering what to do next, the goat's eyelids suddenly flutter. Shaking his head, the old billy wobbles to his feet.

"It's a miracle!" Elmer cries.

Actually, it's a nervous goat. The bullet whizzing by his head must have made him faint.

"Here," Elmer says, handing me his rifle. "I'm never going to use this again."

"But what about your boss?" I ask.

"I'm thinking about going into politics," Elmer says.

A trigger-happy lawyer, with no sense of direction, who can't tell a buck from a billy goat. . . .

I've voted for worse.

Jackie O.

"**M**ORE WINE?" CHARLIE SHOUTS.

Before I have time to answer, Charlie leaps up from the table, cups his hand over his mouth, and bellows toward the kitchen.

"HEY SIEGFRIED, WE'RE SUCKING AIR OUT HERE!"

Sweetie and I are at a dinner party given by our old friend, Charlie, and his fiancée, Twinkie. We're probably the only people in the room who didn't arrive by limo, and I suspect, other than Charlie and Twinkie, we have almost nothing in common with these people. But, in the spirit of cultural diversity, we plan to eat the native food, drink the native drink, and make a sincere effort to let them assimilate us into their tax bracket.

Charlie made his fortune in earplugs. After working eight hours a day next to a buzz saw at the sawmill, Charlie figured out when he crammed a wad of bubble gum in each ear, it kept the sound out.

A few modifications, like removing the spit, and Charlie had a patent. Two years later almost every industrial plant in the United States started requiring ear protection and Charlie was rich as Midas before the age of thirty. Unfortunately, he was also a tad bit hard of hearing by this time.

"BUT WITH THESE BABIES," Charlie yells, tapping a hearing aid with his fork, "I CAN HEAR A FROG FART IN FARGO."

The woman next to me grimaces. This woman could be the poster girl for the slogan, "You can never be too rich or too thin." Her spindly little arms make E.T. look like Mike Tyson, and if her lips were pinched together any tighter we'd have to feed her intravenously.

"*Nouveau riche*," she mutters.

"Nice ring," I say, making an effort to bond with the natives.

"It was one of Jacqueline's," the woman says.

"Jackie O.?" I say, leaning in for a better gawk.

"*Jacqueline . . . Kennedy . . . Onassis*," she enunciates, as she slides her hand out of view.

Excusez moi.

Sweetie fared much better with the seating arrangements. Two miles down the table, he's sitting next to our hostess, Twinkie, a model with the I.Q. of a swizzle stick, but mammary glands that could end world hunger. Twinkie is best known as the Better Beaver Chainsaw girl.

Siegfried finally shows up, wearing a tux and an attitude.

"Thank you," I say, as he fills my glass.

Eyes narrowed to slits, Siegfried snaps his chin—and the bottle—into the air, and storms back to the kitchen. Apparently, what differentiates the mere rich from the filthy rich is a servant who treats you like dirt.

While the rest of the party retires to the parlor for coffee, I head for the powder room. This is no easy feat. There are planets smaller than Charlie's house. I've been after him for years to put mileposts in the halls.

Finally, swinging into the doorway, I come to a dead stop. There, in a pile on the Oriental rug, are Siegfried and my delightful dinner companion, Jackie O.

"Can't you knock?!" Jackie O. demands, as she pulls herself together.

Not like these two. Their bony bodies were clanking together like a couple of bamboo windchimes in a hurricane.

Stiff lipped—and I suspect this to be the only part of the boy retaining starch—Siegfried grabs his tray and flies past me, with Jackie O. in hot pursuit.

The good news is, the rich put their pantyhose on one leg at a time, just like the rest of us.

Resolution

SWEETIE NEVER MAKES NEW YEAR'S RESOLU-
tions. According to him, he reached perfection back in '89 and there's just no place left for him to go.

"I'd like to tell him where to go," Leila says.

"You'd be breaking one of our resolutions," I say.

Leila and I see ourselves as diamonds in the rough. We figure, with some buffing here and polishing there, we have the potential to be real gems. It's just a matter of a little behavior modification, and maybe a few sessions with an exorcist.

So, at the end of each year, we sit down at her kitchen table with pen and paper and reflect on those teeny tiny little flaws we feel are preventing us from being the people we know we really are—a mix of Mother Teresa, Margaret Thatcher, and Sharon Stone, with Martha Stewart's organizational skills.

"Do you know that Mother Teresa's order of nuns take a vow to own nothing but a change of habit, a plate, and a bucket?" Leila asks.

"A bucket?" I ask.

"What modesty. What humility," Leila says, thoughtfully sipping her coffee. "Think of the tens of thousands of lives she's touched."

"What kind of bucket?" I ask, dipping a chip. "You mean like, galvanized?"

"Do you have any idea how few women have won the Nobel Prize?"

"Do you suppose she gets a special bucket?" I ponder, licking cheesecake off my fork, "or is her bucket just like everyone else's?"

"She's lived in India since she was eighteen, surrounded by disease and despair, serving the destitute, knowing her life is little more than a Band-Aid on an open wound."

". . . I bet they carry their change of habit in it, like a little bucket suitcase . . . and they probably wash their plate in it . . . and you could turn it upside down and sit on it . . ."

I'm starting to wonder how on earth I've made it this far in life without a bucket.

"Resolution number one," Leila declares. "We will donate one evening a week to charity."

"O.K.," I say. "But not Tuesday or Thursday. I've got Muscle Sculpt."

"Wednesday's out. Chuck does my roots."

"Friday . . ." I shrug. "Well . . . it's Friday."

"How about Monday?" Leila says.

"Monday?" I say, biting my lip. "Well . . . I suppose we could tape *The Nanny* . . ."

"O.K.," Leila says, "Resolution number one: we will give more money to worthy causes."

Giddy with the thrill of personal growth and community service, we happily write our New Year's resolution boldly on our paper.

O.K., so maybe "diamonds in the rough" is aiming a bit high. Just think of us as a couple of zirconiums doing the best we can.

Robbed

THE FIRST TIME I GOT ROBBED, THE THIEF STOLE all my underwear.

"Just underwear?" the cop asks as he writes.

"Right," I say.

"What would you estimate the value of the underwear to be?"

I clear my throat. "Uhhh . . . eight hundred dollars?" You think I want a permanent record that I buy my undies where America shops?

"Anything else disturbed?" the cop asks.

"The thief fixed himself a sandwich," I say.

"What kind of sandwich?" the cop asks.

"Roast beef."

"Whole wheat or white?"

"Wheat."

"Mustard or mayo?"

"Would you like a sandwich, officer?"

"Well, if it's not too much trouble," he says, tucking his notepad into his pocket.

Needless to say, my underwear was never found.

I don't understand people who steal. It seems to me it's a lousy way to make a living. Unless they're into women's clothing, there's usually a lot of heavy lifting. The hours stink, and the stress must be incredible. Wouldn't it just be easier to get a job?

"Why on earth do people steal?" I ask my cousin. She's a psychologist. She knows about these things.

"Because they're lowlife leeches on the fast track to Hell!" she thunders.

Don't take this as her professional opinion. Her analysis is a tad bit biased at the moment. She recently got robbed. The thieves took every electrical device in her house.

The last time I got robbed was in Italy. While Sweetie and I were at the beach, three thugs cut the lock out of the trunk of our rental car and robbed us blind: passports, money, credit cards, and clothes. The only thing they left was a pair of Dingo boots.

"Oh, thank goodness! They missed my boots," Sweetie says, clutching them lovingly.

I didn't have the heart to tell him that an Italian stealing American shoes would be like Donald Trump checking into Motel 6.

The Rome police station didn't make it into *Fodor's Guide to Things to See in Italy*, and I can't imagine why. Italian police have the snappiest uniforms you've ever laid eyes on.

The officer who took our statement was, in a word, gorgeous. Black curly hair, shirt open to his knees, and eyelashes that made the papers on his desk flutter when he blinked.

"Where arra yuua fromma?" he asks, with an accent you could lick off a spoon.

"Tennessee," Sweetie says.

"Ahhh . . ." he nods. "Tan-na-sseea."

"You're a country music fan?" Sweetie says.

"Cooontry mu-seek!" The officer spits on the floor beside his desk.

"Tan-na-sseea, home of Jack Daniel's. No?"

"Italy, home of Pavarotti. No?" Sweetie says.

Two hours and a fifth of Jack Black later, Sweetie, dressed in swimming trunks and his Dingo boots, and the entire Rome police force are into the second act of *Marriage of Figaro*, with our officer singing the soprano lead.

Needless to say, we never got our stuff back.

While we're waiting at the American Embassy for new passports, a befuddled priest from Omaha comes in and collapses on the bench in front of us. After saving all his life to come to Rome, he got mugged at the Vatican.

"They even took my cross," he says, staring down at his folded hands.

"Wow," I say. "What kind of person would steal from a priest?"

"A lowlife leech on the fast track to Hell!" the priest thunders.

And that, I believe, was his professional opinion.

The Shower

~~~

I WAS IN LABOR FOR THIRTY-TWO HOURS," LEILA SAYS. "I FInally told the doctor to give me drugs. I'd catch the miracle on video."

We have gathered in my living room for one of the great and ancient rituals of womanhood—the baby shower. As is customary, we come bearing gifts. Feasting on ceremonial foods of fat and sugar, we offer our support by doing our best to experience sympathetic weight gain.

". . . I had stitches from my nose to my knees," Maxine says, sipping raspberry tea.

All of Maxine's kids popped out with five o'clock shadows, including little Suzy, whose goal in life is to become the first female sumo wrestler, if she can get a little weight off.

Meanwhile, Sweetie, draped in cameras and his face intense with adoration, is trying to capture the Madonna in all her glory—bowlegged, swaybacked, and dripping all the various food groups down the front of her maternity top.

According to Sweetie, a woman is never more beautiful than when she's swollen like a tick and about to hatch.

Going into the kitchen to refill the troughs, I find Allison and Kat hovering at the espresso maker. Al's calculator is on the counter and her fingers are flying.

"Do you have any idea how much we're going to spend on this kid?" Al asks, the calculator whirring and printer tape spilling onto the floor.

Al, Kat, and I are the only childless members of our group, which is kind of like being a universal blood donor at a vampire convention.

"If you add up the baby gift, christening gift, high school graduation gift, college graduation gift, and wedding gift . . . amortize this over the life of the little bloodsucker," Al says, hitting TOTAL, "you're looking at a BMW!"

"I don't know," Kat sighs, "sometimes, I wonder if we're missing something."

"You mean besides stretch marks and a fallen bladder?" Al says.

"Can one truly know the fullness of being a woman without experiencing the miracle of motherhood?" Kat ponders.

Al, Kat, and I glance into the living room at our friends. Three of the miracle moms are sitting up and snoring, one is babbling away in baby talk to herself, and Mindy has her finger down her one-year old's throat, trying to dig out the cat food.

With one hand supporting her lower back, and the other stuffing half of a poppy seed pound cake into her mouth, our guest of honor waddles into the kitchen with Sweetie, his camera clicking as fast as it will go, at her heels.

When she sees Al, Kat, and me, it's as if someone flipped her hormone switch.

"I've turned into a Volkswagen!" she squeals, spewing poppy seeds like a leaf blower.

"There, there!" Sweetie says, rushing to her side. "Ancient civilizations worshiped pregnant women! Archaeologists have found clay figurines, swollen with child, dating back thousands of years."

"Really?" she sniffs, consoling herself with a little nibble of cake.

Yeah, and they also worshiped cows.

Talking

ACCORDING TO MY GIRLFRIEND, THE LAST TIME her husband uttered a word was in 1992.

"Really?" I say, watching him channel surf between women's beach volleyball and women's bowling.

"I asked him what he wanted for dinner," she says, taking a sip of coffee.

"What'd he say?" I ask.

"Not fish."

There comes a time in every relationship when as far as the man's concerned, everything that needs to be said has been said. Usually, we women are too busy talking to ourselves to notice, but when we do figure it out, boy, are we mad.

"We never talk anymore," I cry.

Sweetie frowns. From his point of view, this is like getting upset because vinyl siding doesn't need painting.

"We used to talk for hours," I whimper.

Sweetie raises his eyebrow and bites his lip. He knew telling me there was nothing he enjoyed more than curling up with a crispy vegetable platter and chatting about our feelings would someday come back to haunt him.

"I think we need to talk to a counselor," I say, already dialing the number.

Sweetie groans. Oh, great! Now he has to spend eighty dollars an hour talking about why he doesn't talk.

Women need to talk. It's one of our basic requirements, right up there with food, shelter, and a good moisturizer with a sunscreen.

But according to Sweetie, straight guys only talk when they're dating. It's kind of like their mating dance. As soon as they say, "I do," men pack up their tongues and turn on the TV.

In all fairness, I think this whole failure-to-communicate thing really is as much the woman's fault as the man's. Men stop talking when women stop talking about things men want to talk about.

Some women seem to have trouble assimilating this. I'm sorry, but there is simply no way you'll ever lure a man into a rousing conversation about the virtues of cotton over percale sheets—unless you happen to be wearing them.

We women knew this when we were dating. That's why so many of us dated football players. With your standard jock, all you have to do is throw on lip gloss and say, "Wow! They make wine in a pop-top can?" and he'll talk your head off.

But when you date an intellectual, you have to work for it.

When Sweetie and I first started dating, I studied for our dates as if I was cramming to get into Harvard. I'd spend half a day in the library scouring through books. Hot rollers in the hair and nail polish drying, Sis would drill me with flash cards.

Then he'd pick me up and the first words out of his mouth would be, "Nice lip gloss."

But I'm determined not to let us become one of those dried-up couples who sit across from each other in restaurants, eat the entire meal, and the only words exchanged are, "Pass the pepper."

So, once again I hit the books to become astute on the issues Sweetie now deems important.

Waving a pan of warm brownies in front of his nose, I get Sweetie's attention.

"In my opinion," I say, "no other art form has captured the visual beauty of the human body quite like *Baywatch*."

Mall Mauling

WHENEVER I START GETTING THAT MATERNAL yearning, I borrow my nephew. After about two hours, I'm fully prepared to donate all my female organs to science.

Kid and I are standing in front of the mall. For the third time he walks toward the double doors, only to skid to a stop right before he smashes into the glass. With a blank look on his face, he tries stomping the ground with his size two Air Jordans.

"What does it say?" I ask, pointing to the sign on the door.

"Puh . . . puh . . . puh . . . uh . . . uh . . . uh . . . sssh . . . sssh . . . sssh," Kid reads phonetically.

Grabbing the handle, I push the door open and Kid struts past.

"What kind of door do you have to push open?" he grumbles under his breath.

This is what four hundred dollars a month of private schooling buys you, a kid who can surf the Internet, but doesn't have a clue how to open a door.

Huddling beside a couple of mannequins, I decompress Kid for mall entry. Unzipping his little jacket, I snatch mittens off each hand and stuff them into his pockets. When we get to his Nike cap, I'm at a loss. Kid points to my knapsack, so I cram it in.

"O.K." I say, bending down into his little face, "I do not want you out of my sight. Do I make myself clear?"

I learned my lesson the last time I was in charge of Kid. He disappeared on me at the grocery store, and right before I graduated from hysteria to blubbering idiot, the produce man wheeled out a cart of cabbages with Kid on the bottom rack. If an understanding mother hadn't held me back, Kid would be coleslaw right now.

"What if I have to . . . you know?" Kid asks.

"Hold it, or I watch," I say. "It's your call."

Allowing children to have input into decision-making is necessary for social development.

"Alright," I say. "To the food court."

Kid takes off like a bloodhound.

I'm guessing that, of the six years Kid's been on this earth, at least five of them have been spent at the mall. He was potty trained at Dillard's, and his first words were, "What do you mean, the card's maxed out?"

After circling the food court for fifteen minutes, we finally manage to stake a claim on a table.

"Plant your butt in the chair," I say, dropping Kid's burger and fries in front of him.

Gasping, the mother next to us glares at me like I just bit Kid's head off and am crunching on it.

"What?" I say.

"You said a nasty word!" Kid whispers.

Standing up, he bends over and points to the GUESS label on his jeans.

"You mean *butt*?!" I say. "Says who?"

"Says everybody," Kid shrugs, drowning his fries in catsup.

I hate it when they change the rules on me. I vividly remember Mom saying, as she exfoliated my tongue with a toothbrush and a little Lava, that the "A word" was nasty, and "b-u-t-t" was the word of choice. Suddenly, my entire upbringing seems on very shaky ground.

About this time, a Chicken McNugget skids across our table. Kid and I trace its flight path back to a man and woman loudly exchanging words that Mom would have pulled out the Comet for.

"Are you and Uncle Sweetie going to break up?" Kid asks, munching on a fry.

"Why?" I ask. "Do you know something I don't know?"

Kid gives this some thought. "Do you know long division?"

"It depends," I say. "Have they changed the rules?"

Suddenly, a glob of stromboli splashes down for a landing.

"Good heavens!" the mother next to us says. "What on earth is going on?"

"She's mad because he said she has a big behind," Kid explains matter-of-factly.

"Well," the mother mutters, "I certainly hope she told him to kiss her donkey."

Aunt Maude's Clock

WHEN THEY FOUND MY GREAT AUNT MAUDE she already looked like the mortician had done his deed, with her hands folded across her chest, a faint smile on her face, and a half-empty bottle of Jack Daniel's on the nightstand.

"Coma," the doctor diagnosed, "most likely induced by a stroke."

Aunt Maude's children, Uncle Jimmy and Aunt Lillian, had been predicting this very thing for years.

"She smoked," Aunt Lillian said.

"And drank," Uncle Jimmy added.

And, at seventy-six, she went dancing on Saturday nights at the Senior Citizen's Center, played bridge for money on Wednesdays, and every spring drove to Memphis for her pilgrimage to Graceland.

"It's gaudy as hell," she'd say, "but everyone needs a little religion."

With Aunt Maude tied to tubes and the Angel of Death reading a year-old *People* magazine outside her hospital door, Lillian and Jimmy took it upon themselves to get Aunt Maude's affairs in order. So, they sold her house and divvied up the spoils.

All this went fairly well until they got to the grandfather clock. The grandfather clock was the only thing in the house that might qualify as a family heirloom. Aunt Maude's grandfather had brought it over from the old country, which, for all Lillian and Jimmy knew, was Virginia.

Apparently, one of the requirements for the *nouveau riche* to move up the ladder to real riche, is a family heirloom. Making a fortune in real estate only gets you on the waiting list.

Lillian and Jimmy, having both been born with the urgent need to climb, went to war over Aunt Maude's clock. Lillian, having access to a truck, won.

While Jimmy was yelling at his wife that "THIS is why I need a truck," Lillian was having dead bolts installed on all her doors.

A call from the doctor called a temporary truce over their mother's deathbed.

They arrived to find Aunt Maude perched under the NO SMOKING sign, a Tiparillo in one hand, a cup of coffee in the other, and the remains of two eggs, sausage, and biscuits on the tray in front of her.

"Best rest I've had in years," Aunt Maude declared, blowing a billowing puff of smoke into Aunt Lillian's pale face.

While the doctor sputtered something about the consequences of combining whiskey with prescription sinus pills, Aunt Maude did her morning stretches.

For the next two years, having no place else to go, Aunt Maude was passed from Jimmy to Lillian as tolerance would allow, and the healthy environments soon took their toll on her. First they took away her Tiparillos, then her whiskey, and finally her car.

"You could break a hip dancing," they insisted.

Eventually Aunt Maude's days were reduced to watching Andy Griffith reruns and winding the grandfather clock.

One night, while Lillian and Jimmy were sleeping, Aunt Maude, in her final act of independence, died. If the doctor didn't write as cause of death, "her children's love" on the death certificate, he should be arrested for falsifying records.

Having nothing left to bequeath, Aunt Maude's last handwritten will and testament simply read, "Don't bury me in pink."

"It was her best color," Aunt Lillian said, as she arranged a spray of pink roses over her mother's folded hands.

When Lillian arrived home from the funeral she sensed something was missing. That afternoon she realized it was the sound of ticking. The grandfather clock had stopped. And it has never worked since.

She's called in several people who know about clocks to take a look at it. Each time they say they can't find anything wrong with it, but they can't get it to work either.

After a while the silence must have started to wear on Lillian. First she moved the clock from the living room to the den, then from the den to the guest bedroom. Then she tried to move it to Jimmy's.

"I'm sure mother would have wanted you to keep it," Jimmy assured her.

It's uncertain what will become of the clock. None of Maude's grandchildren seem interested in it. Jimmy Jr. has his eye on his father's '54 Lincoln Premiere and Lillian's girls have already started arguing over which one will get her house. But the clock remains unspoken for—and silent.

The Actor

G REAT PARTY, HUH?" WESTON SAYS.

Flashing a frozen Pepsodent smile, the woman stares at Weston like he's transparent, then keeps on walking.

"Man, I hate actresses!" Weston mutters into his glass.

Despite twirling his BMW key chain and slipping in as much lawyer-speak as possible, Weston's been batting zero all night.

Meanwhile, eyes narrowed to slits and sucking on a cigarette like it's his life support, my Sweetie's getting meaner by the minute. The only thing worse than being in a room full of beautiful aspiring actresses and batting zero, is being in a room full of beautiful aspiring actresses and not being able to swing at all.

Sweetie, Weston, and I are at a movie screening. One of Weston's clients knows somebody who knows somebody, and here we are. Where I come from, this is called crashing the party. Weston, being a lawyer, calls it networking.

Feeling a hand on my arm, I turn to find a friend I haven't seen in years.

"Come!" Mimi says, kissing me on each cheek. "I want you to meet my soon-to-be ex-husband—*the actor*."

Taking me by the hand, Mimi pulls me across the room to where, surrounded by a captivated audience and perched on an elevated black leather director's chair, sits the actor. This guy is so macho, his capped teeth came stained.

". . . so Sly says to me, try the steamed dumplings. And I figure, hey, he should know. It's his restaurant, right?"

Mimi's soon-to-be ex, the actor, takes a bored drag off his cigarette, meditates on the track lights for a minute—which is the closest to enlightenment this boy will ever get—then fixes his stare on me. One can't help but notice, he's wearing eyeliner.

"You're *somebody*, right?" he says, pointing his cigarette at me. "Wait, don't tell me . . . the Sundance Film Festival . . . no, Cannes . . ."

By this time everyone in the room is staring at me, and I have this uncontrollable urge to break into "Old Man River."

Finally, leaning over, Mimi whispers into his ear, and the actor's corneas frost over like he just discovered that the paté is really Spam.

Based on the look on his face, the room goes back to not doing whatever they were not doing before, and my fifteen seconds of fame buzz by so fast, I have razor burn.

"You have to admire the guy," Weston is saying, when I rejoin my fellow nobodys. "Tossing job security to the wind, he stepped off the path of least resistance and went for his dream. . . ."

"He never had a job to toss," I say, grabbing a stuffed mushroom off a waiter's tray as he flies by. "Mimi supported him for ten years, until he got his first big break, then he dumped her."

"Marrying an aspiring actor is like buying a Yugo," Sweetie says, blowing smoke out of the side of his mouth. "Chances are you won't be mentioning either of them in your will."

Suddenly, Weston's eyes blaze. I haven't seen him this fired up since he defended a ninety-pound cat-killing rottweiler, using self-defense as the plea.

Knocking actresses out of the way like top-weighted bowling pins, Weston comes to a stop in front of the actor.

"I'd like to review the facts," Weston says. "Did, in fact, a woman support you for *ten years*? And did you, in fact, on the exact day you were cast in a blockbuster movie, tell her to 'hit the road'?"

Leaning forward, Weston stares into the black outlined whites of the actor's eyes.

"Exactly, how does one get a woman to do that?"

Surviving the
Magic Kingdom

$\sim$

D URING A MOMENT OF GODMOTHER DELIR-
ium, I promised Cortney I'd take her to Disney World. So, I
closed my eyes, waved my magic MasterCard, and now Sis,
Cortney, and I are sitting on a Delta goose, waiting to fly.

Sweetie's inside the airport waving *bon voyage*, and I'm
beginning to suspect he's not that sorry to see us go. He's just
popped a bottle of champagne and three black-haired Puerto
Rican girls gyrate like tops around the Caribbean band's steel
drums.

Meanwhile, I'm sitting on a plane writhing with
munchkins from around the world. At the rear, twenty
Japanese kids are singing the Mickey Mouse song in Japanese.
Their voices are starting to get a little hoarse, but judging by
their perfect pitch and synchronized harmony, they've been
practicing since Tokyo.

In the seat next to us, a prim woman and her two grim
kids, sit backbone straight. The kids are obviously adopted or
the result of Immaculate Conception. This doll's oven has
never had the pilot light lit.

Bending down, Snow White lifts the gingham towel on
her picnic basket, and I'm expecting the Blue Bird of Happiness to come flying out. Instead, she pulls out two Ziploc

bags, labeled "Plane Snacks," and hands them to each kid. Being a quick study, I scratch a couple of Tic-Tacs off the bottom of my knapsack, pull the hairs off, and pass them to Cortney.

We've been sitting at the gate an unusually long time, and Sis is starting to fidget. She's got an unlit cigarette in her mouth and is trying to give it CPR.

Inside the airport, two of the Puerto Rican girls grip a silk scarf in their teeth as Sweetie does the limbo.

"Ladies and gentlemen . . ." the overhead speaker cracks.

Up ahead, three young businessmen are checking out our seats as if they'd like to huff, puff, and blow us off the planet.

". . . this flight has been overbooked, and we're looking for volunteers to take the 4 P.M. flight."

"Yeah, right," every adult on the plane snickers.

". . . and we'll give each passenger a fifty dollar travel voucher for their trouble."

A hush falls over the plane.

". . . one hundred dollars . . ."

By this time, Sweetie's stuck to the airport window like a tree frog.

". . . two hundred dollars . . ."

Sneaking a sideways glance, I check out Snow White. Her lips are pencil thin.

I look over at Sis for guidance. She's dissecting a cigarette with her fingernail file, trying to figure out a way to inject it.

". . . three hundred dollars . . . EACH."

Inside the airport, Sweetie's waving two florescent orange flags and screaming, "GET OFF THE PLANE!"

It doesn't take a Japanese calculator to do the math. Nine hundred dollars would go a long way toward paying for the trip. And it's only six hours.

I look down into Cortney's upturned face. Someday, she

will be a strong and beautiful woman, but when I think of her, this will be the face I see.

As the three young businessmen brush animal crackers out of Snow White's former seats, one of the Puerto Rican girls holds Sweetie's head in her lap while the other two fan.

"I think Uncle Sweetie's sick," Cortney says, as our plane pulls away from the gate.

If wishes do come true, it'll last about four days.

The Perfect Man

B ETSY IS MARRIED TO THE PERFECT MAN.
Howard cooks like the Galloping Gourmet, cleans like Molly
Maid, and there's no place on earth he'd rather be than an
over-priced bed and breakfast. Sweetie calls him "Howie, the
Happy Eunuch."

"Oh, Howard, everything is simply lovely!" Leila and
Mindy gush.

Being the perfect man, Howie loves to entertain.
Tonight's theme is Greek. Marinated lamb sizzles on the spit,
"Yanni at the Acropolis" synthesizes on the CD player, and a
replica of the Parthenon, molded out of goat cheese, crowns
the candlelit table.

"You show me a man who plays with cheese," Sweetie
huffs, "and I'll show you a guy so whipped he spreads
like Parkay."

As Howie pulls Betsy's chair out for her, our guys fight
over the seats with a view of the TV.

"Do you suppose she found him like this," Mindy whispers, as Howie snaps Betsy's napkin open, and spreads it in
her lap, "or did she have him professionally trained?"

The dining room overlooks the steaming hot tub, that's located in front of the crackling fire, that's installed in the sunroom, that faces the pool—all of which Howard built.

"Howard installed *and* refinished the hardwood floors, *all by himself*," Leila, eyebrows arched, says to her husband, the doctor. There's a Doc-in-the-Box on every corner. What are the odds of finding a good floor man?

"After dinner," Betsy announces, "Howard is going to teach us a Greek dance he saw on public television."

Mindy's husband rolls his eyes knowingly from Sweetie to Doc. Further credence to this theory that, not only is Howard a wimp, he's a socialist wimp.

Rolling out a little cart, Howard begins to prepare Caesar salad at the table.

"Betsy, that is the cutest outfit" Leila says, as Howie rubs the wooden salad bowl down with fresh garlic.

"Howard picked it out for me," Betsy shrugs.

"And your hair, it's fantastic," Mindy says, as Howie tears the romaine into perfect bite size pieces.

"Howard trimmed it this morning," Betsy says with a yawn.

Leila, Mindy, and I look at each other. He shops, he chops, he dices. Maybe she ordered him from Ronco.

"So, Howie, who's your pick for the World Series?" Sweetie asks.

"Howard doesn't watch baseball," Betsy says.

"What does he watch?" Mindy's husband asks.

"Howard doesn't hunt, fish, watch, or play any kind of sports," Betsy says proudly.

I guess it goes without saying he doesn't smoke or chew.

Doc dips a Dorito into the Parthenon, Mindy's husband

slams down a shot of ouzo, and Sweetie fires up a cigarette. The guys smell something fishy, and it's not just the anchovies in the salad.

"Let me get this straight," Sweetie says, blowing smoke to the ceiling. "Howie likes to cook, clean, shop, and sculpt goat cheese, and when you say jump, he uses a pole. Am I right here?"

"That's it in a nutshell," Betsy says, checking out her reflection in her soup spoon.

"Former gymnast?" Sweetie asks.

"I can touch my nose to my toes," Betsy purrs.

Fat

Every January I stand in front of my bath-room mirror and survey the damage. After the nausea has subsided, I place my hand on the scale and take a solemn oath.

"I will run ten miles a day, eat only raw carrots, and drink my weight in water," I say with total conviction.

About thirty minutes, a ham sandwich, and a sixteen-ounce bag of nacho flavored Tostitos later, I contemplate my alternatives.

"Hello," I say. "I was wondering if you could give me a rough estimate on the cost of liposuction."

"Exactly which area of your body are you concerned with?" the nurse asks.

"Oh, you know," I say, "that irritating little sack of fat between my chin and my ankles."

Actually, my cheeks are a bit plump too, but I figure I can work that off.

How did I let myself get into this condition? It seems like only yesterday I could slip into size-six jeans while movin' on down the highway. Now, I couldn't slip into a size six with WD-40 and a crowbar.

But I'm fully prepared to place the blame where it belongs.

"This is all your fault!" I say.

"What?" Sweetie says, looking up wide-eyed and innocent.

"Look at me!" I say, taking a turn, which is no easy feat in a room with furniture. "Just look at me!"

Of course, I immediately regret saying this, because the fact is, he hasn't really looked at me in a decade or two, and if I had just kept my mouth shut, things would have been just fine.

"WHOA!" he says, spitting Famous Amos cookie crumbs across the room.

And there lies the problem. Sweetie can eat anything he wants and thinks "work-out" is Japanese for "negotiation."

"Excuse me, but did you actually move?" I wheeze, as I pull my second set of fifty crunches.

"Dropped the remote," Sweetie says, between spoons of Häagen-Dazs.

A few years ago, I thought "Fat Gram" was a rap singer. I drank whole milk like a kitten, didn't think twice about slathering mayo on a toasted cheese sandwich, and still had a stomach you could bounce a quarter on. Nowadays, I can't walk past the dairy section without my thighs curdling like cottage cheese.

But it's a new year. A time to begin again.

With fist raised to the sky and carrot juice on my breath, I stare into my bathroom mirror and make this pledge: "As God is my witness, if Demi Moore can get up at 4 A.M. to work out, so can I! If Demi Moore can do one thousand sit-ups a week, so can I! If Demi Moore can make twelve million dollars a flick—she can afford liposuction."

What Are Friends For?

Yesterday, Rosie got a postcard from the twenty-two-year-old vixen who ran off with her husband. Say what you will about the girl. How many wanton, husband-stealing hussies remember to send a thank-you note?

"She thought I'd like to know he was all right," Rosie says, twisting her wedding band," and she hopes we can be friends . . ."

"Friends?!!" Maxine says, busting open a bag of wedding cookies and spilling them into a bowl. "Who does she think she is, Jennifer Aniston?"

"May she choke on an enchilada," Leila says, sniffing a bowl. "Is this dip?"

Frowning, Maxine scoops a fingerful, tastes it, and then throws the bowl in the sink. When you drink coffee at Maxine's, you chase it with penicillin.

"He always wanted to go to Acapulco," Rosie sighs, carefully folding her hands in her lap so she doesn't touch anything.

Rosie never eats or drinks anything at Maxine's. Of course, Maxine doesn't take it personally. We are, after all, talking about a woman whose husband's pet name for her was Lysol—chilled not stirred.

"So, why didn't you guys ever go to Acapulco?" I ask, as I fight the cat for the creamer. Once you've seen what's growing in Maxine's refrigerator, cat spit seems like spring water.

"Well, one year we needed new carpet," Rosie shrugs. "Then, last year, we had to stencil the kitchen . . ."

By the time Rosie gets down to sketching the design on her potholders, *I'm* ready to run for the border.

"If you completely identify with a man," I whisper to Leila, "does that mean you're less of a woman?"

"No," Leila whispers back from behind her coffee cup, "but you can bet any woman who chooses Stainmaster over Acapulco is sushi in the boudoir."

Don't get us wrong. We all love Rosie like a sister. We'd each give her a kidney if she needed one. Of course, she wouldn't take it.

But let's just say, when it comes to sex drive, Rosie seems to have an ignition problem.

"How could he leave me for her?" Rosie asks, holding the postcard in both hands. "She has absolutely no idea when to use a comma."

"Oh yeah," Maxine mumbles, blowing a hair off a Cheeto and popping it in her mouth, "there's been many a cold shower taken over a girl's ability to punctuate."

"Rosie . . .," I say, taking a deep breath.

"Don't go there," Leila mutters, as she fishes something out of her coffee, checks for movement, then flicks it on the floor.

Rosie is staring at me with the eyes of a lost beagle pup.

". . . you were always too good for that scum sucker," I say.

Sometimes, the last thing a friend needs is the truth.

Pink Rollers

LAST NIGHT I DREAMED ABOUT RICHARD GERE.

"Well, I certainly hope he didn't see your hair like this," my hairdresser says, as he lets a limp strand drop to my shoulder.

While Sergie and I may place a slightly different emphasis on *mon coiffure*, the one thing we do have in common is we both love Richard Gere.

"So, there's a knock on my front door," I say. "And there he is, Richard Gere."

"Tell me," Sergie says, closing his eyes and pinching the bridge of his nose, "when someone asks what your secret to hair care is, do you say 'Tide'?"

"Richard's BMW was broken down in my driveway, and he wants to use my phone."

"How convenient," Sergie quips, as he snips at my split ends.

"That's why they call them dreams, Serge."

"Indeed."

"I step back and Richard walks inside."

"Is he wearing his black Armani cashmere coat, French tailored shirt, and pleated, but snug around the hips, black pants?" Sergie asks nonchalantly, as he turns my chin from side-to-side to check my bangs.

"And his collar was open."

Sergie sucks in a breath. "Be still my heart."

"While I'm looking through the phone book for a wrecker service, Richard walks around my living room, casually looking back over his shoulder at me."

"You didn't offer him anything to drink?" Sergie says in disbelief. "Girl, were you reared by hogs?!"

"Then he says to me, 'I don't believe we've been properly introduced. My name is Richard Gere.'"

"Earthy, yet *so* continental," Sergie swoons.

"'Mr. Gere,' I say. "I'm familiar with your work. You first reached prominence in *American Gigolo*, then went on to star in *An Officer and a Gentleman*, with Debra Winger, *Pretty Woman* with Julia Roberts, and my personal favorite, *First Knight* with Sean Connery."

"If he doesn't get an Oscar nomination for *First Knight*," Sergie says, drowning my cowlick with gel, "I'm going to write someone a VERY nasty letter."

"Richard looks at me, long and hard."

Sergie fans his face with a hairbrush.

"Richard says, 'I've never met anyone quite like you'."

"You knew, sooner or later, he was bound to get bored with exquisite bodies and flawless faces," Sergie says.

"Then our eyes meet, and it was like nothing else needed to be said."

"Honey, I'm right here with you," Sergie says, holding my hand.

"Slowly Richard walks across the room toward me."

"Yes . . ." Sergie says breathlessly.

"And the next thing I know, we're playing Scrabble," I say.

"Scrabble?" Sergie says dryly, throwing my hand down. "You've got Richard Gere marooned in your living room, and the most creative thing you can come up with is SCRABBLE?!"

"Good girl," a voice calls out from the stall next to us.

Frowning at each other, Sergie and I cautiously glance around the corner of the partition. A tiny blue-haired grandmother with a head full of tightly wound pink rollers smiles at us.

"Nothing gets a man worked up like a rousing parlor game!" she says.

Bowl Game

MY GIRLFRIEND LIVES IN A HAUNTED HOUSE. For more than fifty years, every night at exactly midnight, every toilet seat in the place slams down with a fury. In a house with three men and four bathrooms, this gives the term "bowl game" a whole new meaning.

"It's definitely a girl ghost," I say.

"Absolutely," Leila says.

"Must have had one too many baptisms in the great porcelain font," I say, sipping my coffee.

"Nothing perturbs a girl more," Leila says.

"Wonder why ghosts never haunt your basic ranch style?" I say.

"Inadequate closet space would be my first guess."

Sweetie and Leila's husband, feeling a discussion about ghosts is beneath them, lean against the fireplace mantel and engage in that never-ending and profound debate—"push versus riding" lawn mowers.

Generally speaking, I think men have a real problem with things they can't see, touch, or trade on the New York Stock Exchange. Women, on the other hand, having spent thousands of years contending with men's egos, have no trouble whatsoever grasping the concept of the "supernatural."

"He won't talk about the ghost," Leila says, looking over at her husband.

"Maybe acknowledgment of the supernatural would blur his definitions of life and death."

"Nah," Leila says. "He's afraid it'll depreciate the house."

What can I tell you? Leila's husband is a doctor.

"The reason the toilet seats slam down is, a fragment of the geological plate is shifting, causing a momentary tilt in the structural foundation," Doc interjects, using his best "I am Doctor, I know everything" tone. This from a man whose profession once declared leeches a medical breakthrough.

"Yeah," I huff. "A tilting foundation is really going to raise a prospective homeowner's comfort level."

"Well, it raised mine," Doc mutters.

"Maybe the toilets aren't vented right," Sweetie says. "Maybe, gas builds up, then sucks the lids down."

Sweetie knows a lot about gas, so I don't feel qualified to dispute this one.

"You know," Leila says, "rather than argue *why*, wouldn't it be more constructive to figure out *how* to stop the slamming?"

"Right," I say, taking her lead. "Say, for instance, the seats were left in the *down* position, the ghost wouldn't be able to slam them."

Suddenly Sweetie's pupils turn into dollar signs.

"*A toilet seat that returns to the down position when flushed . . .*" Sweetie says breathlessly to Doc.

"I smell *patent*!" Doc declares.

"Why not just put the seat down when you get through with it?" Leila says.

"Where's the money in that?" Sweetie frowns.

While the boys scurry off to the laboratory to build a better lavatory, Leila throws another log on the fire, and I shift ever so slightly for consistent broiling. The stomach's full, the coffee's fresh ground, and the toes are toasty. If the ghost gave Swedish massages, I'd feel I'd died and gone to Club Med.

"Well," I say, "we solved that one. What's next on the agenda?"

"I've never been able to get him to pick up his dirty clothes," Leila says.

I mull over the possibility of "dancing dirty clothes."

"Too quiet," I say.

"We could have the ghost rustle the newspapers he leaves on the floor."

"Nah," I say. "Rustling newspapers have been done to death."

Suddenly, Leila and I are distracted by dishes rattling. As the grandfather clock strikes midnight, Sweetie's and Doc's coffee cups, saucers, spoons, and dessert plates zip down the mantel, hurl across the room, and smash into the wall.

Wide-eyed and hearts pounding, Leila and I grab each other.

"SHE WANTS US TO TEACH HIM TO PUT HIS DIRTY DISHES IN THE DISHWASHER!" Leila and I chime in unison.

There's just no limit to what can be accomplished when you put three women in a huddle.

Life

THERE'S NOTHING LIKE BUMPING INTO AN OLD friend to put your life into perspective.

"Paula," my friend shouts from across the mall.

"Allison," I yell back.

Kiss, kiss. Hug, hug.

"You look great," I say.

"And you . . ." she looks me up and down, "just got out of a wind tunnel?"

"So what have you been up to?" I ask, ignoring the last dig because basically I do look like a hairball the cat spit up. Hey, we're at the mall. It's not like I was expecting to run into Richard Gere or anything.

"Well, let's see," she says, "I've finished my double-doctorate. I walked across Australia with Aborigines. I took the family business international last year and tripled the family fortune. And I'm engaged."

She holds out her perfectly manicured hand with a rock the size of a Porsche 911 on her ring finger.

"And you?" she asks.

"Well . . ." I say, biting my lip in thought. "Yesterday I bought suet for my birdfeeder. Today I'm shampooing the carpets, and tomorrow I'm exfoliating my face."

"Your mother must be very proud," she says.

"Ha, ha," I laugh. "You're not going to call her, are you?"

The sum total of my life's accomplishments could fit on a postage stamp and still leave room for Elvis. I'm average and I know it. Being average seems to be a progressive disease. The more your friends progress, the more average you become.

One solution is to associate only with people who do even less than you do. Unfortunately, by the time you've sunk to my level this is unlikely to happen—unless, of course, you're able to strike up a relationship with a baby chicken.

Actually, being average is not so bad, except when you run into your highly successful friends, or on Saturday mornings when your mother calls.

"Good morning, darling," my mother says. "Have you amounted to anything yet?"

"No, Mother. I'm still your little lump of clay," I say.

I have one of those '60s mothers. She never hoped I'd marry a doctor. She hoped I'd cure all disease and make the entire medical field, as we know it, obsolete.

"Well, sweetheart," my mother says, "I certainly don't want you to feel pressured, but, of course, you realize when Beethoven was your age he was dead."

"I think you mean Mozart, Mother," I say. "When Mozart was my age he was dead."

"It's good to see the twenty thousand we spent on your education was not entirely for naught," mother says, her tone as dry as cornstarch.

I have this theory that we average people know the secret of life. Take it slow. Stop and smell the cheeseburgers. Catch a movie now and then and call it culture. Overachievers really aren't that happy. How could they be? All that work-work-work, go-go-go, achieve-achieve-achieve.

So, Allison and I are saying goodbye at the mall, and I can't help but ask her about this.

"Come on Al," I say. "Sure you're well-traveled, rich, and about to marry the perfect man. But are you really happy?"

"Yes," she says without missing a beat. "Absolutely."

Well, so much for that theory.

Skin the Cat

ONE OF THE BASIC LAWS OF LIFE IS, YOU NEVER appreciate what you've got until somebody else wants it. This is especially true with men.

It is absolutely amazing what a little competition will do to a girl's perspective. The minute another woman starts circling overhead—*Voila!*—right before your eyes the man in your life is transformed from something just slightly above a road kill into the mold from which male perfection is cast.

This is especially true if the vulture happens to be a girlfriend.

"So, how is that incredible hunk of a man of yours doing?" Allison asks, as she cuts me a slice of my favorite pie.

"Who?" I frown.

"Sweetie, you silly girl."

"Oh," I say, still a little disoriented by that "incredible hunk" thing. "He's O.K., I guess."

"I hear his business is really taking off," Allison chats nonchalantly, as she sprays a two-inch layer of whipped cream on top of the pie.

"Yeah," I say.

"Looking good too," Allison says.

"Hmmm . . ." I shrug, mouth stuffed to capacity.

"So . . . still no ring on that finger?" Allison slips into the conversation like a hot knife into butter.

I stop mid-chew. Exactly where is this conversation going, I wonder. I check out Allison's hand. Her engagement ring is gone! Good golly! I've been dealing with a free agent!!!

O.K., so I'm slow, but this cat still has claws.

"Allison," I hiss, back arched, eyes narrowed, "this mouse has been cornered. Go catch your own."

"Now, now," Allison purrs, as she slathers on lipstick, "the trap with the best cheese wins."

Who would have thought an '87 Honda could break the sound barrier?

I blow into Sweetie's office like an Israeli Green Beret, fully equipped and ready for combat.

"What are you doing here?" Sweetie asks.

"I just couldn't go another minute without you, my love," I say, as I position his shoe on my knee, spit on the toe, and buff it to a brilliant shine. "So, tell me all about your day."

"You talking to me?" he frowns, looking behind him.

"Well, of course I am, my prince, my love, my reason for being. Nothing interests me more than . . . oh, you know . . . whatever it is you do."

"Do you need money?" he asks.

"Oh," I sigh, "is there no end to your generosity? To think I have found a man who is not only brilliant, cultured, and successful, but is also the standard for which altruism can be measured. . . ."

"This morning you said dating a tick would be less irritating," he says.

"A girl can change her mind, can't she?"

The minute one woman gets that hungry look in her eye for your man, the whole female population seems to start salivating. Walking down the street with him is like nibbling on a Big Mac in a lion's den.

You also start to notice little things you never noticed before, like the only available men left in the world have less facial hair than you do, and that there are a lot of women out there who make you look like the Pillsbury doughgirl.

The competition is vicious. You can't help but wonder, how in the world did you manage to snag such a great catch in the first place?

"Sweetie," I say, "what exactly made you choose me over all the other girls you were dating?"

"You begged," he says.

"Oh yeah, I'd almost forgotten," I say, biting my lip. "By the way, do you remember my girlfriend, Allison?"

"The rich one with the knockout body? Yeah, why?"

"Did I ever mention she used to be a man?"

There's more than one way to skin a cat.

Winners and Losers

SUNDAY, ALLISON'S FIANCÉ GOT MARRIED TO a waitress he met on a business trip to Alabama. We were all shocked.

Poor Al went through the usual rainbow of emotions. We had to hand-feed her for about two days, teach her how to hold her head up again, then confiscate her Smith & Wesson. Then she *really* got mad.

Nothing infuriates a girl more than breaking a guy in for another woman.

"I taught that rodent everything he knows," Al says, as she feeds his pictures into her paper shredder. "Before me, he was just potential in a bad suit!"

It's a familiar story. Girl finds a nice fixer-upper guy, sands off the rough spots, primes him, puts on a new coat, and suddenly he's a hot property. Then some hermit crab moves in, and before a girl can say "palimony," the title's been transferred.

To add insult to injury, I got an invitation to the wedding. Being the good friend that I am—that and the fact I put weddings right up there with scooping the solids out of the litter box—I had planned not to go. But Allison insisted. In fact, she drove me.

"Have you got everything?" she asks, as she shoves me out the door of her BMW onto the church steps.

I check my bag . . . notepad, mini-tape recorder, Polaroid. I nod.

"I don't want to see your face without details!" Al snaps, then slams the door and floors it.

After the reception we are to rendezvous at a coffee shop within walking distance of the church. Well, walking distance if you're a horse. Furthermore, my happy little jaunt takes me through a simply delightful part of town. I must say there is nothing quite as enlightening as having your exact worth—in dollars and cents—called out to you from a slow moving Ford Escort.

By the time I finally get to the coffee shop, Al is having a hissy.

"Where have you been?!" she snaps.

Using an espresso spoon as a shoe horn, I break the vacuum between my shoe and foot. Immediately a blister the size of a baby waterbed pops up on my heel.

"WELL?" Al yells, and every head in the place turns our way.

I'm beginning to suspect we've had just a tad bit too much café and not enough au lait during the interim.

"Well . . ." I begin.

"I want the truth!" Al demands.

No she doesn't.

"Yes, I do," she insists.

I hand Al the Polaroids of the happy couple.

"She isn't as pretty as me," Al says, as she studies the glossies. "She isn't as successful . . . SHE ISN'T AS RICH!" Al looks up at me bewildered. "Was he drugged?"

"I think it's because she makes him *feel* good-looking, successful, and rich," I suggest gently.

Al sighs. "I never could get that humble act down."

"This girl deserves an Oscar," I say.

Lifting her chin and her cup of latté, Al makes a toast. "To the girl with the better mouse trap," she says, ". . . and the RAT she caught in it."

"Here! Here!" I say as our cups clink.

Of course the really good news is, if she takes after her mother, in two years the blushing bride is going to make the Goodyear Blimp look like a mini-marshmallow. But I'll save that tidbit for a rainy day. Judging by the expression on Al's face, the rainy season has just begun.

Light of My Life

LOUSY . . . CHEAP . . . PIECE OF . . . GARBAGE!!!"
Sweetie snarls.

Sweetie and I are surrounded by two acres of screws, reflectors, bulbs, and every plastic part that's ever been extruded. Apparently, TO BE ASSEMBLED is Korean for MINING COPPER TO MAKE WIRE.

After feeling my way to the back door for four months, I've decided it's time to shed a little light on the situation. If it were left up to Sweetie, I'd sleep in the car.

"Screw!" Sweetie says.

"Phillips or slothead?"

"Phillips."

"Half-inch or three-quarters?"

"Half."

I slam the screw in Sweetie's hand like a surgical nurse.

Watching a man perform domestic duties really makes a girl feel warm and fuzzy.

That and the fact that there is nothing sexier than a guy with a screwdriver—except, of course a sweaty guy with a screwdriver.

"Hey!" Sweetie snaps, slapping my hand away. "I'm trying to concentrate here!"

If turning a screwdriver requires this much brain power, one shivers to think what flushing a commode must do.

Biting his lip, Sweetie tries to match fixture parts to the little drawings on the instructions, which are carved on clay tables in ancient hieroglyphics. His hair is tossed, and there's a little wisp of chest hair sprouting through one of the worn holes in his T-shirt.

"Geeez!" Sweetie groans, shaking me off his leg. "How am I supposed to work under these conditions?!"

Fifteen minutes of assembly and Sweetie has turned into Norma Rae.

Having finished Assembly Phase, Sweetie prepares for Installation Phase.

Crawling under the deck, he stretches out on his back in two inches of mud.

Now, he's really in a good mood.

"Measure!" Sweetie barks.

Aligning the measuring tape, I mark the step at the midway point.

All I can see of Sweetie are his legs sticking out from under the deck. He looks like the Wicked Witch of the West after Dorothy's house fell on her.

Suddenly, I notice a tiny sliver of his ankle exposed between his jeans and his Timberlands. It's like dangling a filet mignon in a lion's den.

"Wire!" he calls.

A little growl escapes through my extending canines.

"Screwdriver!"

The line between civilization and animal instinct snaps. Eyes narrowed to slits, I move in for the kiss. Just as my lips come in contact with flesh, white light flashes before my eyes, my whole body shudders, and I feel fairly certain I am having an out-of-body experience. That, or my eyes haven't caught up with my body, which is sailing toward the rhododendrons.

"Hmmmmm . . ." Sweetie says, fanning smoke away, ". . . must have flipped off the wrong electric breaker."

It is night and we're still sitting on the deck. Other than replacing a little charred wood around the electric plug, our work is complete.

Five of the eight step lights actually work—if you count intermittent flashing. The balcony light, installed upside down, is sending a halogen beam to the heavens. A Cessna, circling the roof, awaits clearance to land.

Sometimes Appetizers
Are Enough

$\sim$

MEN ARE LIKE FOOD. YOU'VE GOT YOUR APPE-
tizer—a flavorful, yet rarely satisfying tidbit, meant only to hold
you over until the main course arrives. And you've got your
main course—which at its best is not only well-balanced and at-
tractively displayed, but leaves absolutely no room for dessert.

Eating can be tricky business. Sometimes a girl can get
into the habit of filling up on appetizers before the main
course arrives, and it's up to her friends to guide her back to
a healthy diet.

Translation: When your girlfriend is dating a dip, it's up to
you to tell her to lick those fingers clean and eat her peas and
carrots like the rest of us.

"Paula," my girlfriend Elizabeth says, "this is Slice. Slice,
Paula."

Slice rolls his eyes away from a SLAM video on MTV and
glares up at me from the couch.

"Does it understand English?" I whisper to Liz.

"Does it matter?" she whispers back.

While Liz goes for drinks, Slice shows me his tattoos.

"And this one . . ." he says, holding up his T-shirt and
pointing to his flat and well-sculpted abdomen, ". . . is a prey-
ing mantis. Like, I really dig the mantis."

"And exactly why would that be, Slice?" I ask.

"After they mate," he says seriously, "the girl mantis bites the guy's head off."

"And you think that's cool?" I ask.

"Actually," Slice leans toward me and slowly licks his lips, "I'm intrigued by the juxtaposition of violence and the act of reproduction."

"Gee," I say, giggling nervously. "Aren't we all?"

After Slice leaves for his job at the rendering plant, I decide to have a little talk with Liz.

"Lizzy, other than his blinding good looks and underlying hint of provocative, albeit twisted, perspective on life, WHAT IN THE WORLD DO YOU SEE IN THAT MAN??!" I ask.

Liz stares at me with this stupid smile fixed on her face like she's been congealed in cherry Jell-O.

"Liz! This is not a drill," I say dryly. "You're dating a man named after a golf swing."

Liz continues to grin at me until I can't take it anymore.

"Alright," I huff. "Be like that. If you want to spend the rest of your life with the *Illustrated Guide to Carnivorous Insects*, so be it!"

"Wow, have you turned into old married woman," Liz says.

I grab my chest and gasp. "Me?" I whimper.

"There was a time when you would have been the first person to defend being swept away by love. But not now, now that you've . . . *settled down*."

"I have not!" I say, managing only a modicum of conviction.

"Mom says Slice is an appetizer, and I should be looking for the main course."

"She did?" I say weakly. "My, what an embarrassingly antiquated analogy."

I leave Liz's house feeling like a balloon with a slow leak. It is a dark day when a girl learns she is no longer the wild and free spirit she once was. When things like stability and a diversified and recession proof portfolio become more important than "hose me down when I burst into flames" passion.

"What's that?" Sweetie asks.

"It's a temporary tattoo," I say, as I apply it to his arm.

"You are so weird!" he says, jerking his arm away. Then, leaning over to check out the package he says, "The Harley Davidson logo isn't that bad, is it? It'll wash off, right?"

Men are like food. Some are appetizers, and some are the main course. But the truth is most men would prefer being treated like an appetizer, and most women need to cut down on the meat and potatoes anyway.

Nag

"SWEETIE, WHY ARE THERE SNOW TIRES IN THE living room?" I ask.

"I don't want them to get wet," Sweetie says, throwing a handful of popcorn at his mouth and missing.

Sweetie maintains his ideal weight by only hitting his mouth twenty-five percent of the time.

"Well, that's a relief," I said dryly. "For a minute, I thought you were turning the sofa into an all-terrain vehicle."

Before I can suck the words back, Sweetie's eyes roll up to the ceiling, as he contemplates the marketing possibilities of a NASCAR couch. "Why train the little woman to fetch, when you can drive to the fridge in half the time, with none of the complaining?"

In every relationship, one person is bound to be a tad bit neater than the other. Let's just say that, in our relationship, Sweetie would be snug as a bug living in a dumpster.

On top of the fact that you could set up a food bank under Sweetie's chair, Sweetie is an information freak. He subscribes to three newspapers, half a dozen newsletters, and seventeen magazines—all of which he wants open and within arms reach from any vantage point in the house. When friends drop by unexpected, I tell them we're paper training flying squirrels.

I know I shouldn't complain. As maintenance goes, it doesn't take that much to keep Sweetie happy. Feed him, water him, change the papers in his cage. . . .

Evolutionists maintain that mankind's ancestors swung in trees. Sweetie evolved from hamsters.

"Sweetie," I say, as I untangle the cat from the web of computer cables and check for breathing, "I thought you said your laptop computer, desktop computer, scanner, modem, Internet service, and fax machine were going to make this a paperless society."

Sweetie doesn't hear me. He's too busy tearing out articles he wants to save, and filing the little bits of ragged paper between the rails on the stairs.

In the early days, we had a real labor division problem in our relationship. Eventually, we found ourselves in a whine-whine situation.

"You never put the dishes in the dishwasher!" I whined.

"Yeah, well you never put gas in the car!" Sweetie whined back.

Finally, I decided to initiate a quality assurance program. I begin with the simple concept of Do It Right Today, also known as DIRT.

"You see, Sweetie," I say, extending my pointer, "when you put your glass (*tap*) in the sink (*tap-tap*), then I have to put the glass (*tap*) in the dishwasher (*tap-tap-tap*). If you put your glass (*tap*) directly into the dishwasher (*tap-tap-tap*), it would eliminate the step of putting the glass (*tap*) in the sink (*tap-tap*)—thereby saving time and irritation!"

Sweetie gets up from the table, puts his dirty glass in the refrigerator, and taps out "Shave and a hair cut—two bits" on my forehead. This segues nicely into my discussion about the price of nonconformance.

But a girl either mellows or molds. You just can't make a mink coat out of a hamster's behind. Sweetie has every right to live like a rodent, and I can either like it, leave it, or clean it up.

So, whenever I feel a nag coming on, I use a little secret code to neutralize the hostility.

"Sweetie," I say, as I gather dirty glasses like Easter eggs. "I love you."

Which translated means, "You lazy slob, do I look like your mother!?"

To which Sweetie replies, "I love you, too."

At least I think that's what he's saying. He's siphoning gas from his truck to my car, and the words are a little garbled with the hose in his mouth.

The Nutcracker

S WEETIE," I SAY, "CAN WE GO TO *THE NUT-cracker?*"

"Not unless they're performing it in the nude," he says.

I'd like to fight him on this one, but the thought of Baryshnikov pirouetting in the buff has me somewhat distracted.

The person who coined the phrase "Season of Peace and Love" obviously was not involved in a relationship. While visions of sugar-free sugarplums are dancing in my head, my beloved is standing in front of the mirror practicing, "Bah-Humbug."

Scheduling alone requires a legal mediator.

Last year we ate five meals in six and a half hours, and four of those featured country ham. By 9 P.M. I was feeling real empathy for Lot's wife.

"Christmas Eve, my dad's," he says, "Christmas Day, Mom's."

"We spent last Christmas Eve with YOUR family!"

"Exactly. A precedent has been set."

"I beg to differ," I say, putting on my reading glasses and opening a folder. "If you will recall the 1994 case of 'your grandmother versus my grandmother', you established the 'alternating major holiday visitation rights' decision."

He taps his lip with his pen. "I'll give you Easter for Christmas," he says.

I'll probably agree to this, but a good negotiator always makes them sweat.

Then, of course, there is *gift giving*. Every year the men in our family try to come up with inventive ways not to give gifts. We exchange names. We draw numbers. We do it by age—under eighteen and over sixty get a gift, those of us in-between get eggnog. They modeled that one after the Social Security system. This year I'm still not sure what I'm supposed to do.

"O.K.," I say. "Explain it to me one more time."

"Each letter in your name will be assigned a number between one and ten, vowels are even, consonants odd," he says. "Add the numbers up and divide by seven. Any questions?"

"I don't get a gift again, do I?" I say.

"Nope," he chirps.

I really envy those women who know how to entice their men into loving the holidays. How do you get a man to actually enjoy the hustle and bustle of shopping, lights and tinsel, warm visits with family and friends?

"How are you getting Jerry to go to *The Nutcracker*?" I ask my girlfriend.

"I told him it had soldiers fighting giant rats," Mindy says, sipping her latté.

"Wow! It must be great being married to a cultural void."

"It has its moments."

I'm pretty sure my beloved and I will never agree when it comes to Christmas.

"It's a chick's holiday from start to finish," he says. "Who, but a woman, would come up with a holiday that requires shopping, singing, sitting, and staring?"

"As opposed to a man's holiday, which would require . . ."

"Beer, ball, babes, and bikinis."

Add Baryshnikov to that list, and I might be willing to make some concessions.

The Photo

⁓

IHAVE NEVER HAD A DECENT PICTURE TAKEN OF me in my life. A picture may be worth a thousand words, but mine just sits there and coughs.

Fortunately, it is my philosophy that it's not how you look, it's how you feel in the dark. Unfortunately, there's not a big demand for Braille photography.

Lately, I've felt this incredible urgency to get one decent picture of myself before the skin completely slides off my face.

Must be the age. All my girlfriends are having those glamour photos taken. You know, where two strangers stuff you into black lace garters, stretch you across a fake polar bear rug, then tell you to act natural.

But I'm thinking, do I really want a permanent record of my thigh spread? I decide to call a regular photographer.

I usually judge a photographer by how high he gets my hopes up.

"I never take a good picture," I say.

Taking my chin in his hand, he turns my face from side to side.

"With those cheekbones, those eyes, and that smile?" he says. "Impossible!"

He props me up on a stool in front of a white screen. While he's adjusting the lights, I try to get my lips to unlock.

"Imagine you're eating ice cream," he tells me.

I can relate to that.

"Beautiful," he says, from behind the camera.

The studio is dark, warm, and fuzzy. Hootie and the Blowfish are playing on the stereo and the photographer has an earring.

I start to get into it. I feel myself getting loose. My lips feel fuller and I develop this inexplicable bond to Cindy Crawford. I'm thinking, *swimsuit issue*.

"You're killing me!" the photographer says.

I slowly lick my lips.

I pout.

I am one with Hootie.

"Oh yeah!" he says.

I arch my back and hiss.

I toss my hair.

I fall off the stool.

Driving home I think, that went pretty well. I wonder if he'll make me pay for the stool?

"How'd it go?" Sweetie asks.

"The photographer said I look like Michelle Pfeiffer," I say.

"They have blind photographers?" he asks. "Now, *that's* affirmative action."

Two days later the proofs arrive—with an apology and a disclaimer. We spread them on the kitchen table and a hush falls over the room.

"Well," Sweetie finally says, "this one's not too bad."

I study the picture. It's painful. My face looks like a full moon with feed bags under the craters. One eye looks smaller than the other, and I've been on ski slopes with shorter runs than my nose.

"I look like Uncle Fester," I say.

"Yes, but your gums look healthy."

What can I tell you? I floss.

"So . . . what's with your hair?" he asks.

"I tossed it," I say.

"You *tossed* your hair?"

"You had to be there," I mutter.

My photograph never looks like who I think I am. But I stand by my convictions. It's not how you look; it's how you feel in the dark. That having been said, I'd just like the world to know that in the dark, I feel just like Michelle Pfeiffer.

The Rating Game

OVER THE COURSE OF TIME, THE MALE HOMO sapiens has developed a sophisticated rating system for mate selection.

"A six-pack and the bag it came in," Rolex says, as a woman walks past us.

"So, that means you *wouldn't* go out with her?" I ask.

"Oh, sure," Rolex shrugs, "but only if it was really dark . . . and I was really drunk."

Some of my friends find the idea of guys rating them just a tad bit offensive.

"Gloria says guys who rate women are swine who should be castrated," I say.

"That's because she's a keg," Sweetie says.

"Chugged," Rolex adds.

When it comes to women, Sweetie and Rolex almost always agree. It's my theory that this has something to do with the fact that, being brothers, they grew up in the same sty.

Just when I think I've got the alcohol rate of exchange down pat, we have a two-hour layover at the Dallas airport, and Sweetie changes the standard of currency.

"Nice luggage," Sweetie mumbles into his coffee, as a flight attendant strolls by.

"Compact, yet well constructed," Rolex agrees.

"Did you get a look at that overhead compartment?" the man at the table next to us joins in.

"I'd like to pack my shaving kit in that," Rolex growls.

"So, that means you *would* go out with her?"

"No way," all three guys say in unison, shaking their heads.

"That baby has a lock on her head Houdini couldn't crack," Rolex says.

"By the time you figured out the combination," Sweetie concurs, "the trip would be over."

Translation: The flight attendant is built like a Stealth bomber, but she's "complicated." I'm not exactly sure what "complicated" is, but most guys appear to hate it. How they can surmise a woman is complicated from 150 feet is a mystery to me, but I suspect it has something to do with buttons versus zippers.

"I don't get it," I say. "There seems to be no correlation between a woman's rating and a man's desire to form a long-term relationship."

"Women are like cars," Sweetie says knowingly. "You've got your family car, and you've got your sports car . . ."

". . . which, while sleek and fast," Rolex says, "is very high maintenance."

"While a Porsche will always rate higher," Sweetie continues, "chances are, a guy's going to settle on a nice four-door domestic. It may not keep its resale value, but the price is right and it will get you where you're going."

Excuse me if I'm not thrilled with being compared to a Buick.

About this time a pilot from Air Italia strolls past.

"Nice-a lug-gage," Captain Romeo says, giving me a smile that makes my motor rev.

I roll my eyes toward Sweetie.

"Veerr-rrrooom!" I growl like a Ferrari.

Restoration

ONE OF THE FEW CERTAINTIES IN LIFE IS, WHEN paint is hanging from the house in strips, maple saplings are growing in the gutters, and things have died in the basement and mummified, Man will bolt upright in bed and declare, "If I don't buy a 1952 Chevrolet truck and restore it, I'm going to die."

"It's just a phase he's going through," I assure my girlfriend.

"A phase?" she weeps.

"It's his Restoration Phase," I say. "All men go through it."

"Can't we stop it?"

"Has he bought a monogrammed shop cloth yet?" I ask. She nods.

"The checkered flag is down," I say.

"But what should I do?" she wails.

The only thing a supportive woman can do. Build a fence around it and plant shrubs, because you're going to be looking at that hunk of junk until you're old and gray.

Never mind that he hasn't changed the oil in the car since they built the first Jiffy Lube. Never mind that he can't remember which side of the car the gas cap is on. Suddenly, the man who broke his toe on the basement stairs because he doesn't have time to change a light bulb is going to transform two tons of twisted rust into purring perfection with a mirror finish.

Step 1: The Search.

Restoration Phase makes Man's previous phases look like mood swings. The search for the perfect wreck could take months. And he wants it to. In an ironic twist of fate, suddenly *he* needs foreplay.

We're talking hours spent scanning newspapers and trade magazines, making long-distance phone calls, cruising car graveyards, and taking road trips. When he lugs home a fax machine, you'll know he's on the Restoration Highway without an off ramp.

"Which one do you like?" he asks, cramming a page of one-inch by one-inch black-and-white blurs under your nose.

Just point randomly. He isn't listening anyway.

Step 2: Preparing the Nursery.

One of the few advantages of Restoration Phase is he's going to have to make room for it. This means, if not getting rid of, at least shuffling all the paraphernalia from all his previous phases: Boat Phase, Golf Phase, Fishing Phase, Skiing Phase, and Tour-de-France Bicycling Phase.

Of course there was that brief stint at ballroom dancing, but it's not something you bring up without due cause.

Step 3: Clothes Make the Man.

So you think all a guy needs to pull an engine is a T-shirt and jeans? Silly girl.

A phase is simply not a phase unless it requires coordinating apparel. When he asks you to put French pleats in his coveralls, don't forget to sew the fly shut and see how long it takes him to notice.

Step 4: Bringing Baby Home.

"It's a classic," he says. "I'm going to paint it the original color."

You can only assume he knows the original color by the hermetically sealed microscopic chip of paint he holds in his hand, because the only color you see, other than the Emerald Green grass growing in the floor board, is Chicken Manure White.

"Does it run?" you ask.

"There's only 2,312 of them left in existence," he says.

"Does it run?" you ask again.

"*Road and Track* calls this model the 'Crown Jewel of Trucks'," he beams.

"Does it run?" you ask.

When he whips out his monogrammed shop cloth and starts whistling, "You Can't Always Get What You Want," you know that sucker hasn't turned over since Elvis did Vegas.

Step 5: What's Time to a Grease Monkey?

Going into the second year, you notice the only time he uses the word *finish* is in conjunction with the word *paint*.

"He's never going to finish it, is he?" my girlfriend asks.

"Nope," I say.

"He spends more time and money on that car than on me," she says.

"Yep," I say.

On the other hand, with Restoration Phase you know where he's at, what he's doing, and who he's doing it with. Since rust is not a communicable disease, there's something to be said for that.

The Biscuit

SCIENCE NEVER STUDIES THE REALLY IMPOR-
tant stuff. For instance, how can a woman, who'd rather die
than drink out of an unwashed Coke can, pluck a safety pin
out of a stinking diaper and pop it in her mouth for safe-
keeping? One hates to imagine the forerunner to this evolu-
tionary development.

"Oh gross," I gag.

"Whuut?" Laurie garbles, clutching two plastic duckies in
her teeth.

Laurie hands me the kid—as if I want it—and settles into
the chair across from me. Holding the kid is like holding a
flannel sack filled with warm biscuit dough. You just have to
move your hands in whatever direction it oozes.

"What's another way to say aching loins?" Laurie asks,
staring at her laptop computer.

Along with being a mother, Laurie writes romance nov-
els. All day she changes diapers, pops chocolate malt balls,
and writes about men with bulging biceps and women with
bulging libidos. For Laurie, still recovering from giving birth
to a nine-pound biscuit, this is truly a work of fiction.

Romance is not for the pensive writer. Laurie's contract
calls for two books a year, written under two different pseu-
donyms, at about a dime a word. That means she's pounding
out six love scenes a week, whether she's in the mood or not.

"So, how's it going with you and Sweetie?" she asks.

This is not small talk, it's research. Laurie is always gleaning her friends for material. Plus, if we talk a little shop, she can call this a business meeting and write off the malt balls on her taxes.

"We're doing O.K.," I shrug, proud as punch I can pop a malt ball and balance the Biscuit at the same time.

"Can you be a little more . . . specific?"

"Graphic" is the word she's looking for. Laurie writes level three romance. In level one only the lovers' eyes meet. In level two their lips meet. In level three the only thing that doesn't get sweaty are their brain cells.

Now, normally, I can talk dirty with the best of them. But I have these two baby-blue eyes locked on me like I'm about to tell him that on the weekends, Mr. Rogers slips into black leather and rides with the Hell's Angels. "Can he hear us?" I ask.

"Well, of course he can hear us. He just can't understand what we're saying," she says, studying her computer screen. "Does 'throbbing' have one 'b' or two?"

"How do you know he doesn't understand us?"

"Science," she says.

I look down at the Biscuit. He smiles at me like I'm the greatest thing since Gum Numb.

Science aside, I have a feeling he not only understands what I'm saying, but knows every thought in my head.

To test this I turn my thoughts to the upcoming presidential election.

The Biscuit spits up.

Our scientific experiment is quickly brought to an end by a disturbing odor emanating from the Biscuit's bottom. Grinning, he kicks his fat little legs and squeals.

It may not be scientific, but it's my theory babies are cute so we won't throw them away.

But what do I know? I'm elbow deep in biscuit dough and have a lip lock on a couple of plastic duckies.

It's a Jungle
Out There

∽∽

SWEETIE'S BROTHER IS S.E.C. ALL THE WAY—single, employed, and cute. In Girl World this is the highest rating a guy can get, unless of course he's rich. Then you're playing in a whole new league.

"Can I get you anything?" the waitress asks for the twentieth time.

"I'd really like more coffee," I say, holding up my cup for the twentieth time. I could be face down and gurgling in my tomato basil and this woman wouldn't notice.

"I mean is there . . . *anything* . . . I can do for you?" the waitress purrs as she leans over Sweetie's brother's face.

If this girl's cleavage were shoved up any higher, she'd have to breathe through a straw.

Rolex looks up. Well, his head makes it up. His eyes kinda get hung on the horizon.

"Say 'coffee'," I instruct.

"Coffee," Rolex says.

In the blink of an eye, the waitress disappears in the direction of the kitchen.

I feel like I just wasted one of my three wishes on a cup of coffee.

Apparently, the minute a man becomes available he emits a high-pitched frequency only eligible females can hear. All around us women are glancing at our table, tossing their hair, licking their lips, and rubbing their legs together like crickets.

Sweetie and Rolex have some business to go over, so they're leaving me to take care of the tab.

When Sweetie stands up, I grab him by the collar and lay a big wet one on his lips.

"Marking your territory?" he asks.

"You got it."

Every female in the place mournfully watches as Sweetie and Rolex walk across the restaurant. It's like being on the Titanic and the last dinghy is pushing off without us.

As I'm finishing my coffee, I look up and there's a woman standing at my table.

"Excuse me," she says. "May I sit down?"

There's no doubt in my mind she wants the scoop on Rolex, but she's brought her own coffee, so I like her already.

She fires off her vital statistics, and I must say I'm impressed. She's a corporate lawyer, owns her own home, drives a Lexus, and has a figure to die for. If I were available, I'd marry her.

"I don't normally do things like this," she says.

"Hey," I say. "It's a jungle out there. A girl has to do what a girl has to do."

"You know," she says, as she writes her home phone number on the back of her embossed business card, "I haven't had a date in over two years."

"Two years?!"

"I just feel like, if there's no chemistry, why bother?"

"What's the longest you've ever gone without a date?" I ask the waitress, as she's clearing our table.

"I was in a full body cast for six months one time," she says thoughtfully.

"So, you went six months," I say.

"Heck no," she huffs. "After two weeks I was dating my doctor."

"You pursued a relationship while your body was rigid from the neck down?" the lawyer asks incredulously.

"I could have guessed it'd be something you could relate to," the waitress says, handing me her phone number scratched on the back of a napkin.

It's a jungle out there, and the girl who can start a fire will beat the one who can put them out every time.

Spectator Sports

LEILA USED TO THINK "SPECTATOR SPORT" WAS an oxymoron.

"Only a moron sits on his dead ox watching other people play sports," she'd say.

That was before she spectated the U.S. Men's Swim Team.

"Are you guys ready?" I ask.

"Yeah, yeah," Leila says, blowing me off with a wave.

Leila and Kat are sprawled on the couch, glued to a thirty-six-inch Sony with surround sound, waiting for the men's freestyle swimming relay. On the coffee table is a gallon of Häagen-Dazs, fudge topping, a jar of cherries, a can of real whipped cream, and walnuts in syrup. We're of the school that it's the bowl that makes you fat.

"We're wasting daylight," I say, peering through the Levelors.

"Fifteen minutes," Kat says.

She is, of course, talking "sports time."

Over the years, I've come to realize, that in "sports time," when a guy tells you there are only fifteen minutes left in the half, you might as well throw the teddy in the drawer and blow out the candles.

Acknowledging the agony of defeat, I drop onto the couch and grab a spoon.

We are supposed to be on our way to the lake for a sunset Jet Ski ride. I've got my Aqua Socks on, and the trailer's hitched to the Cherokee. I can feel the wind on my face, the willow flies in my teeth, and the thrill of the near-death experience.

I'm not saying we girls get wild at the lake, or anything, but Leila's Wave Runner does have BROOM painted across the side, and it has absolutely nothing to do with her housekeeper.

"We're wasting our life," I say, throwing my head back and filling my mouth with whipped cream.

"Where's your patriotism?" Leila asks, a cherry stem sticking out of her teeth.

"Do sportscasters take themselves just a little too serious," Kat asks, dipping her finger in the fudge, "or am I all alone here?"

"Oh, my . . . myyy," Leila suddenly says, as the swimmers take their positions.

"How, exactly, do you suppose they get those little bathing suits to stay on?" Kat ponders.

"Slippery little devils, aren't they?" Leila says.

"Do you suppose they shave their *entire* bodies?" Kat says.

"You know," I say, "originally, the Greeks competed in the nude."

We pause for a moment of reverent silence. No one can say we aren't cultured.

"O.K., judges," Leila says, "total up your scores. Americans . . ."

"8.5," Kat says.

"8.5!?" Leila says.

"I just can't get into hairless men," Kat says.

This is something of a revelation. Based on Kat's current love, she has no problem with the brainless.

"I need more information," I say. "When do they get to the evening wear part of the competition?"

Suddenly, Leila shushes us.

Rolling their heads and shaking out their arms, the swimmers step up to their moment in history. And while the hearts of those of us watching pound in our chests, a calm seems to pass over the athletes. It is time and they are ready.

Slowly, their perfect bodies fold into position, arms stretched behind them like wings. The gun goes off and the Olympians soar through the air like glistening dolphins. And as their bodies shatter the glassy surface, Leila, Kat and I, eyes wide, afraid to blink, hold our breath in anticipation . . . but not a single swimsuit slips.

The Tattoo

M INDY TURNED THIRTY TODAY AND DECIDED to take a walk on the Wild Side. Being the friend that I am, I paid for her tattoo.

Of course, our first concern was exactly what does one wear to get a tattoo?

After much soul searching, Mindy opts for a lovely little ensemble that cries out "brunch at the country club," while Beth, sans briefcase and power suit, still looks like Career Barbie.

I have no doubts we're going to be the Belles of the Biker's Ball.

"You got the stuff?" Mindy asks.

Beth hands her a tube of prescription anesthetic ointment the urologist used on her son during some minor surgery. "I can't remember the exact medical term for the procedure," Beth says, while Mindy reads the label. "But basically, they Roto-Rootered his pee-pee, and he never felt a thing."

Evidently, anything that will numb a pee-pee is good enough for Mindy.

"So, what'd your hubby say?" Mindy asks, as she smears ointment on her ankle.

"He said tattoos are trashy, sleazy, and low class," Beth

says, taking the tube and rubbing some on her hip. "It really turned him on."

Giddy with the thrill of naughtiness, we kiss the suburbs goodbye and begin our journey across the great cultural divide.

We're in my car because Mindy doesn't want to drive her BMW on *that* side of town. The girl's about to become a permanent piece of pin cushion art, and she's worried about a dimple in her door.

"Well, this must be the place," Mindy says, peeking out the car window.

Painted across the blackened store front, right above the skull and crossbones, is TATTOOS, BODY PIERCING & BASEBALL TRADING CARDS.

There's a definite sinking feeling in the car.

"You'd think someone would open a tattoo parlor in the mall," Mindy mutters.

Yeah, right between the GAP and Hallmark's Cards and Gifts.

"Well," Beth says, from the backseat, "there is a lawyer's office next door."

I'm assuming this is supposed to somehow heighten the credibility of the establishment, but it's gonna take a lot more than a reputable tattoo parlor to raise my opinion of lawyers.

Dodging broken beer bottles, I park the car by the curb.

"Are you numb yet?" Mindy asks, checking her ankle.

"Can't feel a thing," Beth says, pinching her hip.

"Let's do it!"

The door jangles shut behind us, and it's like we've been transported to *Escape From L.A.* While we girls politely avert our eyes from the pierced and tattooed proprietors, they stare at us like we're wearing edible clothing.

"Take a look around," one of them finally says, pointing to the walls papered from ceiling to floor with designs. "We've got every design in the world . . ."

"We want the Christian fish," Mindy and Beth speed-speak in unison.

". . . except that one," he says.

Apparently, the Baptists haven't ventured into the body art industry yet.

After a brief conference, the illustrated man comes up with a freehand sketch that passes the girls' approval.

"Put her here," he says, patting his knee.

Mindy throws her foot in his lap like a pro.

"Nice pedicure," he says, as he pulls on latex gloves with a snap.

He starts the tattoo thingy and . . . *buzz, buzz* . . . it's over.

Beth, figuring a visible tattoo might not be the best accessory for a CPA career, gets hers on her hip. Modestly wiggling her slacks to bikini level, she stretches out across the chair.

"How's it look?" she asks, straining to see her little fish over her shoulder.

"Looks great!" Mindy and I concur.

"Yeah," the illustrator says, lighting a cigarette. "And the tattoo turned out pretty good too."

Taking Stock

ACCORDING TO SWEETIE, LIFE IS LIKE THE stock market. Some days you're up. Some days you're down. And some days you feel like something the bull left behind.

It is New Year's Eve. Normally, about this time of night, I'm tugging at my control-top pantyhose while some stiff-lipped waiter slides overpriced appetizers in front of me.

But this year . . . I got to plan the party.

"STRIKE!!!!" I scream, as I do a little dance back to the bench.

All around us, balls are thundering down the lanes, and bowlers, dressed in their holiday finest, are feasting on nachos and grooving to the jukebox. You have not lived until you've watched fourteen lanes of bowlers do synchronized bowling to "I'm Proud to Be an American."

"You know," Weston sighs, as he looks around us, "being rich, good-looking, and successful doesn't guarantee happiness."

Sometimes, being friends with Weston is like biting into a Tootsie Roll Pop, only with no chocolate center.

Two burly biker bowlers next to us jump up and bump chests in midair. I figure either this means they're winning, or it's the Hell's Angels' version of CPR.

"I have never been that happy," Weston says.

"Wes," I say. "Shut up and bowl."

It is a little difficult to sympathize with a guy whose idea of suffering is when the laundry goes a little heavy on the starch in his Brooks Brothers boxers.

As Wes mopes up to the ball return, I glance back over my shoulder to check on the rest of our gang.

Leila and Doc are at the snack bar dining on the *specialité du jour*—Weenies of the World.

Sweetie is planted at the pinball machine. A couple of very healthy girls with Dolly Parton hair "ooh" and "aaah" as Sweetie bumps and grinds with each flip of the flipper. Sort of your Chippendale version of the "Pinball Wizard."

Weston flops the ball down the lane, and it hits the gutter before it hits the floor.

"Wes," I say, "there's a guy two lanes over in a neck brace bowling with better form."

"I can't help it," Weston whimpers. "I have nothing to live for."

"Man, what is your problem?!" one of the bikers growls, as he walks toward Wes with his chrome bowling ball in hand.

Visions of Weston's capped teeth tinkling to the floor as a Harley-Davidson bowling ball is rammed into his mouth dance in my head.

"I don't know," Wes says. "I'm just not happy."

"You have more, you do more, you are more," the biker says, "and yet, you feel less?"

"Yes," Weston says.

"You took stock of your life, only to find your portfolio is filled with junk bonds?"

"Yes! Yes!" Wes says.

"I hear what you're sayin', man," the biker nods.

Standing beside Weston, the biker suddenly strikes the pose of Buddha bowler.

"You've got to cradle her like she's made of crystal," he says, ball to his bearded chin.

"Waterford?" Wes asks, following his lead.

"Whatever," he says. "Keep your eye on the prize, and move like you're makin' love in honey. First base . . . second base . . . third base . . . and blow her a kiss goodbye."

As Weston's ball rumbles down the lane, he holds his breath and we all lean forward.

When the ball hits, the pins explode, with only one left rocking. In unison, all the biker bowlers take a deep breath and blow, and the pin drops like it's been shot.

Falling to his knees, Wes throws his arms in the air and belts out the "Star-Spangled Banner." Standing, the biker bowlers put their hands over their hearts (which are tattooed on their chests) and sing harmony.

Life is like the stock market. I've never met a rich analyst.

Vegas

IT IS 5:00 IN THE MORNING, WHICH IS 7:00 MY TIME, which is eight hours past my bedtime. I've had my eyes open so long, I'm having to blink manually.

Sweetie and I, along with around two thousand of our closest friends, are attending a convention in Las Vegas.

Vegas is the ultimate in virtual reality. Out on the strip, a fake volcano erupts on the hour, knights on horseback ride through a pastel Camelot, and girls wearing mini-togas serve you shark-fin soup for $24.95 a bowl, on a floating barge at the Palace. I assume they are real girls, but in Vegas you never know.

Either you love the glitz or you're like our friend John, who's convinced if he looks back as we pull out of town, he'll turn into a pillar of salt substitute.

I, on the other hand, am a risk taker. It runs in the family. There's no telling how much money my grandmother has forked out on stamps, trying to win the Publisher's Clearinghouse Sweepstakes.

Gambling is like life. Some people sweat at the nickel slots, and some people hope their chips will reproduce in their pockets.

Meanwhile, at the roulette table, Harold from Birmingham tosses a hundred-dollar chip on the black. The dealer slowly waves his hand over the board to stop all betting. The little white ball flies around the wheel, bounces twice, and drops into the black like it's coming home.

Wincing with pain, Harold pulls his chips over to the rest of his pile, which resembles the Rocky Mountains. You know a guy's been at the table awhile when he has carpal tunnel syndrome from raking in chips.

All around us, people are feeding slots in a frenzy. Bells are ringing, lights are flashing, and dice are tumbling down the table.

"There's no place on earth like a casino," Harold says, as he places his bet on the thirteen crossroads.

Apparently, he's never taken the kids to Chuck E. Cheese.

Meanwhile, the wheel hits lucky thirteen.

Most people consider it a good night when they can sit at the table long enough to get the seat warm. It is truly awesome to watch someone in the zone. Harold could close his eyes, spit the chips on the table, and still win.

"Some men go for it," Harold says, straightening his stack on the eighteen split, "and some men never take their foot off the brake."

When you're in the zone, you are sometimes bestowed with words of profound wisdom.

. . . and the ball drops into eighteen like a hole-in-one.

By this time, the crowd is two deep and men are standing on chairs to see. Harold's face is glowing, and we can feel the heat radiating from his body.

In total disbelief, we watch as Harold pushes his entire mountain range of chips up the table, not stopping until they're resting on the double zero.

The odds are thirty-five to one.

"Pity the man who dies with his chips in his pocket," Harold smiles, his eyes shining like dollar chips.

With one finger, the dealer spins the wheel and time slows to a crawl. The ball rolls like it's been dipped in honey, and the sounds of the casino grow far away.

Suddenly, the smell of Oil of Olay awakens me from the dream. I look up to see Mrs. Harold, in a pink terry-cloth bath robe and Hush Puppies, foaming at the mouth.

Surveying the situation, she sweeps Harold's chips into her pockets and gives him a look that makes the table cross its legs.

As Harold follows the Hush Puppies away, Sweetie slowly slides a chip on the double zero.

"Pity the man who dies with his chips in his wife's pocket," Sweetie says, lighting a cigarette.

And the room rains chips on the double zero, as each man follows Sweetie's lead.

I can hear the ball bouncing in for a landing, but I can't look. I have ten bucks on the table that says Harold won't look back.

Vinegar

"GOOD VINEGAR IS LIKE A GOOD KISS," DOLL says. "It should make your lips pucker and your toes curl."

"Trash," Sadie mutters.

My great-aunts have come to my kitchen to teach me how to make herb vinegar—if they don't kill each other first. Their grandmother taught their mother, their mother taught them, and now that the stuff costs twenty bucks a bottle at the gourmet shop, I've suddenly developed an interest in family traditions.

"It's too small," Sadie says, squinting at my pot.

"It's big enough," Doll says, throwing it on the stove.

Actually, the pot looks like an Airstream travel trailer next to these tiny cotton-topped ladies. Pin their arms to their sides and you could clean your ears with them.

"The most important thing," Sadie says, taking a sip from a spoon, "is to use good apple cider vinegar."

"Without good herbs," Doll says, "you could use Jack Daniel's and it would taste like bathwater."

"Trash," Sadie mutters.

Sadie believes the Good Lord put alcohol on this earth for medicinal purposes only. This may be the only thing the sisters agree on. Doll keeps a pint of whiskey stashed in the clothes hamper. She makes herself a toddy whenever her nerves need calming, which has pretty much been every day of her adult life.

"The tarragon smells bitter," Sadie says, crushing some in her hand.

"It's perfect," Doll says, throwing it in the pot.

When I was a kid, Doll bought me some real French perfume.

"Always wear the same perfume," Doll would say, dabbing a little behind my knees and in the bends of my arms, "so that whenever a man smells it, he'll be flooded with thoughts of you."

The scent most likely to flood a man's thoughts of Sadie would be BenGay mentholated rub.

"Don't let it come to a boil," Sadie says.

"If it's not hot enough," Doll says, stirring the steaming pot, "it won't set."

The air is so warm and moist, the windows are starting to drip. Tarragon, basil, garlic, and hot red pepper seeps from my pores. I'm pretty sure I could flavor the vinegar simply by dipping my finger in it.

Sadie meticulously positions each herb in her bottles with an old wooden crochet needle, while Doll pokes her herbs in with her finger as fast as she can move. When we are finished, every flat surface in the house is lined with vinegar.

There's no doubt which bottles are Sadie's. Each one is exactly the same, identical right up to the fill line, like they were copied on a Xerox.

You just never know what you'll get with Doll's vinegar. One year she dropped a diamond earring in a bottle and Sadie nearly choked to death.

Doll gave her the Heimlich maneuver and Sadie coughed it all the way across the living room. Other than a little tarnish on the stem, the earring was just fine.

The Wedding

THE TRUTH IS SWEETIE AND I MISSED THE WEDding. We ran up the church steps and were skidding across the foyer just as the blushing couple was coming out the door. Being the people of high moral character that we are, we ducked into the stairway until we could inconspicuously mingle with the crowd on their way out. Sweetie says it was the best wedding he ever attended.

We were, however, right on time for the reception.

"All I said was, elope and I'll give you half of what this shindig is going to cost up front," the father of the bride tells his captive audience. "Then, if you're still married in three years, I'll give you another ten grand."

The night is young. The disc jockey yawns as he seamlessly strings one piece of elevator music to another. The men in the crowd are starting to loosen their ties and the sound of women breaking the vacuum on their new shoes fills the room.

"So, how many of these guys have you known in the biblical sense?" Allison asks, as we help ourselves to punch.

Interesting choice of words coming from someone who makes a conscious effort to avoid doing things by the book.

"One . . . two . . . three . . ." Allison counts, scanning the crowd like a surveillance camera.

Standing side by side, we size up the room.

"Now, is *that* the groom's father?" I ask.

"Groom's mother's third husband," Al says. "The groom's father is standing between his second wife and the bride's step-mother . . . or maybe it's her godmother. Actually, I think she's both."

I always fade when the conversation turns to who begat whom.

Suddenly, the groom's father looks our way. If looks could melt, they'd be mopping Al and me off the floor right now.

While I'd love to believe his lust is a reflection of our intellect, refreshing wit, and the timelessness of our beauty, I feel fairly certain any fresh carcass would have sent this buzzard circling.

About this time the bride makes her way to the punch bowl, and one can't help but notice she's hysterical.

"Honey, every girl gets cold feet at her first wedding," Al says, handing the bride a cup of punch.

"Did you see the men on his mother's side of the family?" the bride wails. "They're all bald!"

Allison and I check out the room. Now that the bride has brought it to our attention, it is like being at a family reunion of the Coneheads.

"Wait, wait, wait," Al says. "That's not the groom's biological mother. He was adopted. For all we know his biological mother was as hairy as an ape."

"You know," the bride says, "he does have hair on his back."

"To hairy backs," Al says, refilling all our cups.

Dabbing the bride's eyes, we send her running happily back to her baboon groom.

"I'll stand guard while you snatch our gifts off the table,"
Al says.

"You got it," I say.

There's nothing like a wedding to renew your faith in the
bonds of holy matrimony.

Whitewater

~◦~

FIRST LADY HILLARY RODHAM CLINTON WAS ON the cover of *Time* magazine recently, and the question on everyone's mind is, who does this woman's makeup?

"I've seen cadavers with warmer skin tone," Leila says.

"One certainly wouldn't want her teeth near any main arteries," Sergie says, holding his hands up so he doesn't drip hair hydrator on the page.

"And her skin texture," Leila says, squinting for better scrutiny. "Grapefruits have smaller pores."

"Toner is a girl's best friend," Sergie quips, working Leila's scalp into a lather.

Newsweek, the *Wall Street Journal*, and CNN can take polls 'til the cows come home. If you want to know what America is really thinking, get a perm.

Hair dryers at the salon are frying and every other lavender-walled booth is stuffed with women in various stages of torture. Smoke billowing from a pesticide plant would be less toxic than the fumes steaming off the heads of these women.

"What kind of press secretary would let Hillary leave the house without lipliner?" Leila muses, shaking her head.

"The woman has no upper lip," Sergie snips, rolling his eyes. "What's to line?"

"So, what do you think about Whitewater?" I ask, scanning the article.

Sergie and Leila look at me.

"You mean like rafting?" Sergie asks.

"No, no, Serge," Leila huffs, slapping him on the arm. "It's that trailer park thing Hillary did in Arkansas. Right?"

Somehow the Whitewater scandal just hasn't caught the imagination of the beauty seeking crowd. It lacks that one essential element—sex.

Now, if Hillary had been caught dressed in drag and having a grand old party in the Oval Office with Newt, we'd have something we could sink our teeth into. But illegal commodity trading, stock transfers, conflicts of interest . . .

Yawn.

Americans want their scandals scantily clad and rare in the middle. White-collar crimes are too fuzzy. Heck, most people can't understand their phone bills, much less insider trading.

Then there's the fact that Hillary is just not a fun person to gossip about. Let's face it, the Terminator was less driven than this woman.

Still, since a pile of my tax money has gone into this investigation—and they're asking for $600,000 more—I'm at least going to try and understand what she's being accused of.

"The truth about Whitewater . . ." I begin, determined to read the entire article aloud. Sergie and Leila groan, but Leila's roots have ten minutes to go, so I have a captive audience.

About halfway down page two, Leila and Sergie's eyes glaze over.

"Hillary is innocent," Leila declares.

"Absolutely," Sergie says.

"And exactly how did we come to this conclusion?" I ask.

"It's obvious," Leila says.

"Obvious," Sergie echoes. "I ask you, if Hillary had made any money off Whitewater, would she be wearing that suit?"

Wigging Out

Iᶠ YOU WANT TO KEEP THE STEAM IN A RELATION-
ship," Wanda says, "I have one word for you: *wigs*."

I'm sitting at Wanda's Wonderful World of Wigs, wash-
and-wear hair for the woman in a hurry (or the victim of a
bad home perm). I've got a mass of feathery red curls on my
head and I look like an endangered species.

"Men go crazy for redheads," Wanda says.

"Sweetie calls redheads 'peel-and-eat shrimp'," I say. "By
the time he gets past the hassle, he's not hungry anymore."

Four women draped in plastic aprons look up from their
Cosmo's. There are more heads dripping red in this place
than the war-wounded in *Gone With the Wind*.

Wanda jerks the rooster off my head.

Normally, I'm not a wig person. I'm more your "what you
see, is what you get" kinda girl. But today, when I go to pick
Sweetie up from his business meeting, I am going to "pick
Sweetie up"—if you catch my drift.

"Same bed, different dreams, huh kid?" Wanda winks.

You can tell Wanda anything. She's a registered beautician
and cosmetologist, which is just like talking to a priest, except she lectures you on cuticle care.

"Here's a nice little number," Wanda says, holding up a white Styrofoam head with blonde wispy tendrils dangling to the floor.

This would be an excellent choice if you were buck naked and standing in a seashell.

"Women buy these so fast," Wanda says, using a pick like a Wave Runner. "I can't keep them in stock."

"Name one who doesn't write off pasties as a tax deduction," I say.

Wanda hangs Aphrodite in the corner and plops a sleek little black wig on my head.

Humming *Light My Fire*, Wanda pins the synthetic scalp to my head, stands back and gasps. I glance around the room. The other patrons, perfectly plucked eyebrows arched, are staring at me with mouths gaping and unadulterated copycat lust in their eyes.

"Wrap her up," I say.

As my two-inch heels click on the marble floor in the hotel lobby, heads turn like I'm a Wilson tennis ball at Wimbledon. From the top of my perfectly coifed simulated hair, to the tips of my fire-engine-red nails, I am the essence of steamy seduction. Honey, I'm so hot, you could light candles with my toes.

I'm wearing the black wig, a new slinky little black dress, and a major Sharon Stone attitude. My mother would need dental records to identify me.

Like a cat stalking her prey, I check out Sweetie in the lounge from behind my Ray-Bans. He's perusing a *Wall Street Journal* and sipping a frozen frappacino. Poor baby, little does he know he's about to be devoured by a lethal man-eating vamp.

Slowly, I slide into a cool leather wingback at the table next to him. At the perfect moment, I clear my throat.

Sweetie looks up. Sweetie looks down. Then Sweetie slowly looks up again.

I smile a haunting Mona Lisa smile.

"Did you remember to get the oil changed in the truck?" he asks.

Wild Man

~

YESTERDAY MY GIRLFRIEND CALLED TO TELL me the magic has gone out of her marriage.

"He's just not the man I married," she cried. "He's changed."

"Let's see," I say, "when you met him he had hair to his butt, rode a Harley, and was a bouncer at the Hard Rock Cafe. Now he drives a Volvo station wagon, has a haircut only Donna Reed could love, and sells insurance for Allstate. Yeah, I'd say that qualifies as a change."

Another classic case of "WOMAN TRANSFORMS WILD MAN INTO COCKER SPAINIEL."

Women just don't seem to get it. You can't dress Tarzan in Dockers, straddle him with two car payments and a thirty-year mortgage, and still expect him to beat his chest and swing through the Broyhill at night. It ain't gonna happen.

Yet, over and over again, like crazed mad scientists, women just keep trying. The results are often tragic.

Take, for example, my friend Danny.

Danny basically had three areas of expertise: hunting, fishing, and football. You know the kind of guy I'm talking about. He drove a Jeep, slept in the buff, and drank Budweiser with his cornflakes.

Then he married Jane.

"Danny?" I ask, "Is that you?"

Danny looks up from his needlepoint.

"Paula," he says. "Would you care for a cup of tea? We have a simply lovely selection. May I suggest a nice jasmine with a touch of honey?"

"Are you feeling O.K.?"

"Heavens yes," he chirps. "Jane has me on a multitude of vitamins and a non-fat, alcohol free diet. Do you mind if I fold clothes while we talk?"

"Danny!" I shout, taking him by the shoulders and shaking him, "come back to me, man! Remember guns, Jeeps, and *Monday Night Football!*?"

"Ffff . . . ffff . . . ffffootball," he sputters, a flicker of life returning to his eyes.

About that time Jane walks in.

"Dan-Dan," Jane says, "my widdle pea pod, why haven't you wallpapered the living room, like I asked?"

"Ffff . . . ffff . . . fffootball," Danny stutters.

Jane gasps. "Danny! I told you never to mention that word in this house!"

Jane's narrowed eyes roll accusingly my way. "You!" she hisses, pointing at me.

"Jane! Jane," I plead. "Look what you've done to him! You've turned a stallion into a carousel pony."

"It's simply the initial stage of transformation," Jane states clinically. "Once he's reached the appropriate level of submission, I plan to gradually return him to an acceptable level of self-reliance."

"But Jane," I beseech, "no woman has ever successfully taken a man this low and brought him back!"

"If it doesn't work," Jane shrugs, "at least I'll get a lot of things done around the house."

Since the dawn of womankind, women throughout the ages have been drawn to the Wild Man. He's dangerous. He's gorgeous. He's exciting.

Like spiders, we weave our webs. Go to any gathering and listen to the Siren's breathy call.

"Oh, I've *always* wanted to ride four thousand miles across the Australian desert on the back of a three wheeler! There's nothing I love more than grit in my teeth, going to the bathroom in hand-dug trenches, and temperatures that could boil an egg in the sweat of my palm, except of course wild, uninhibited sex . . . with my husband."

Blink. Blink.

The Wild Man falls like a proud, ferocious lion into the percale-covered pit. The minute the poor guy says, "I do," the woman clearly states, "Not in this house, you don't!" And the roar fades from the jungle.

Six months after the wedding the woman cries, "The magic has gone out of our relationship."

And our former Wild Man, after putting in a ten-hour day at the office, not including the commute, his voice now a high mezzo-soprana, squeaks, "Anything you say, dear."

The Workaholic

SOMETIMES A GUY GETS CONFUSED. HE STARTS to think work, ambition, and the almighty dollar are what life's all about. And it is a woman's job to guide him back to what's really important—women.

There is no mistress like a guy's work. I'd rather go up against Sharon Stone than a man's job. At least I've got the same equipment—albeit somewhat depreciated.

Women walk a very narrow line, or at least it seems that way when you have hips designed for childbearing. On the one hand it is important to encourage and nourish your man's career. On the other hand, when a guy gets that lustful look in his eye, then reaches for his computer's on-off switch instead of yours, you've got a problem.

But how does a girl compete with the thrill of rising costs and falling revenue? How can she lure her man away from the rush of upward trends and group performance?

She does it the old-fashioned way. She whines.

"Sweetie, this weekend, could we . . ."

"No can do," he says, snapping his newspaper open. "Gotta work."

"But it's Thanksgiving weekend," you say.

"Not in Tokyo," he quips from behind the paper.

It's times like these that separate the women from the girls, and nothing more clearly defines the distinction than our manipulation skills.

Crying—baby stuff. Blackmail—been there, done that. Negotiation—where do you think you are, Congress?

No, the real proof that a woman has "arrived" is her agility at a very advanced and tricky strategy that is way beyond the capability of the average female.

Silence.

After about five minutes, the corner of the newspaper will fold down and he will cautiously peer over.

Nonchalantly, drink your coffee and continue to look at the pictures in your "I Can Dream, Can't I? Handbook"—*Cosmo*.

"I said, I have to WORK this weekend," he says.

"Hmmm," you say. "Is there any chance of your getting home early?"

"No way!" he says.

"Good," you say under your breath.

"What?" he says, closing his newspaper like an accordion.

At this point, lay your *Cosmopolitan* on the table, opened to an article with a title like "Weekend Affairs with Luscious Latin Lovers," and get up to refill your coffee.

While at the sink, practice a little Spanish. "*Sí, me gustaría.*"

Take a sip of coffee, close your eyes, tilt your head back, and moan like you mean it.

For an added touch, mambo back to the table. Then smile a mysterious smile, slowly lick your lips, and set your thoughts on simmer.

Stocks may rise and stocks may fall, but you can bet your sweetie will be clinging to you like 100 percent Lycra for at least the next forty-eight hours.

A man's work is important to him. He needs to end each day with a sense of having created something, having left his mark. But a corporation can't hold your hand and watch the leaves fall. And you can't make spoons with a BMW.

Behind every successful man, there is a woman. And behind every successful woman there is a little psychology—and a "Spanish Made Easy" Berlitz tape.

Cats Are People, Too

A<small>CCORDING TO SWEETIE, DOGS ARE REAL PETS</small> and cats are future roadkill. He feels it's no coincidence that *cat* rhymes with *splat*.

So, when I show up with one of our feline friends, the fur hits the fan.

"Exactly which part of the sentence, 'NO, I don't want a cat because I *HATE* them,' did you not understand?" Sweetie asks.

"I sensed some ambivalence," I say, cooing into the box.

"Were you dropped as a child?"

"What should we name him?" I ask.

"Dead Cat Walking," Sweetie says, without a trace of ambivalence.

Sweetie glares down into the box.

"What's wrong with his tail?"

"He's a stubby-tailed Manx," I say defensively.

"He looks like John Wayne Bobbitt," Sweetie says, crossing his legs.

"Don't listen to Daddy," I say, reaching down into the box, only to jerk my hand back up after our little fur ball of joy nearly takes my finger off.

Sweetie takes a drag off his cigarette and exhales out the side of his mouth.

"Shouldn't he wear a little hook on his stub?" he says.

"No smoking in the nursery," I say.

This being our first baby kitty, I, of course, walked away from the pet store with a truckload of accessories.

"According to the *Kitty Kat Kare* book," I read, "the KatKan, with dual charcoal filters, is the Mercedes of litter boxes."

"What is this?" Sweetie asks, dangling a stuffed mouse by the tip of its leather tail.

"It's an educational toy," I say, as I assemble the modular carpeted scratching compound.

I decided against catnip. I was afraid it might lead to stronger drugs.

It is 2 A.M. and Cat is ripping through the house like he has a bottle rocket tied to his stub. After about his third stampede over the bed, Sweetie turns on the light.

"It says cats are 'nocturnal,'" I yawn, reading from the *Kitty Kat Kare* book.

"Nocturnal," Sweetie nods. "This is some sort of payback, isn't it?"

"Maybe if you read to him—"

"READ TO HIM!?" Sweetie screams.

Cat sits in Sweetie's lap, staring at the open book. I can't help but notice, Cat's posture is perfect.

"Love to eat them mousies," Sweetie reads, rocking. "Mousies what I love to eat. Bite their little heads off, nibble on their tiny feet . . ."

"Don't you think that's a little violent for bedtime reading?" I frown.

"He's a boy," Sweetie snaps. "Don't coddle him."

The next day Sweetie and I are just sitting down to dinner, when Cat decides to join us. Lightly landing on the table, he drops a little treat between the green beans and the broiled chicken.

"It's a dead mouse," Sweetie says, bending over the limp little carcass.

"It's his gift to us," I say, reading from the *Kitty Kat Kare* book. "We're supposed to praise him."

"Oh great," Sweetie mumbles. "We're living with Jeffrey Dahmer."

Chest puffed and one paw resting on his kill, Cat stares at us.

"Ohhhh . . . isn't he precious!" I say, going for the camera. "His first kill!"

"Does it concern you," Sweetie asks, pushing his plate away, "that if we were a little smaller, he would eat us?"

"He gets that from your side of the family," I say, as the flashbulb goes off.

Bunny Hop

⌒

MOM NEVER GOES ANYWHERE WITHOUT HER photo album. When it comes to celebrating the moments of her life, misery loves company.

"And here are the girls in their Easter bonnets," Mom says, tilting her photo album for the women at the table behind us to see.

I have no idea how old this picture is, but Sis was still in training pants.

"They were such a joy—when they were young," Mom says, turning the page.

On that note, Sis lights a cigarette.

Sis and I are having lunch with our mother at one of her many charity meetings. At the head table, Madame President bangs her spoon against her fruit-tea glass, and the room immediately comes to order. Nikita Khrushchev could learn from this woman.

"First," Madame President says, peering over her glasses, "I want to thank Lois Lester for today's lovely decorations."

The ladies clap, and Lois takes a modest bow in front of one of her ceramic catfish centerpieces. Other than the rhinestone eyes, the detailing is quite remarkable.

Madame President turns the meeting over to Madame Secretary, and as the minutes from the last meeting are being read, a woman slips in through the side door. One can't help but notice, she's stacked like the great pyramids.

"Oh, there's Sugar," Mom says, stretching up from the table and giving a little wave across the room.

"Late as usual," Sis notes.

Tardiness is not the first thing that comes to mind. Let's just say Sugar's dress is cut so low, she could have a mammogram without unbuttoning a button. In Sugar's defense, it would take an awning to cover those babies.

"In her younger days, Sugar was a rabbit," Mom says, as she picks parsley off her congealed salad.

Most of the time, I have no idea what my mother is talking about. It's like being at the United Nations without a translator.

"You know," Mom says, totally exasperated, "fluffy tail . . . big ears . . . three-inch spiked heels and a push-up bra."

"Sugar was a *Playboy* bunny," Sis translates, blowing smoke out the side of her mouth.

"One of your best friends was a *Playboy* bunny?!"

I'm stunned. It's like finding out Mother Teresa and Madonna get together and paint each other's nails.

"Miss June, 1963," Mom says, peeling open a cucumber sandwich and salting it.

Now, there's a photo album that would draw a crowd.

"Missed Playmate of the Year by this much," Mom says, making a little gap between the cream cheese on her thumb and index finger.

In the Bunny Business, you can lose by a hair.

"So, after being a bunny, what did she do?" I ask. I've always wondered what happens to bunnies, once they lose their tails.

"Oh, she did what we all did back then," Mom shrugs. "Got married. Had kids. Settled down into a life of thankless servitude."

Spotting us, Sugar starts bouncing her way through the tables in our direction. It's like dueling basketballs.

And you better believe heads are turning. If looks could kill, Sugar would be rabbit stew.

"They're just jealous," Mom says, nibbling on her sandwich.

"It's understandable," I say, as I watch Sugar dribble our way. "While you were patting out hamburgers and matching socks, Sugar was going to movie premieres and drinking champagne on yachts."

Mom stops chewing.

"But you'll always have us, Mom," I say, patting her limp hand.

"Sugar's daughter is an aeronautics engineer," Sis says, smashing her cigarette out in the remains of her quiche. "She helped design the space shuttle."

It figures Sugar's kid would be a whiz at lift and thrust.

Funeral

⁓

OF THE ONE HOUR AND THIRTY-SEVEN MINUTES that the funeral lasted, two minutes were devoted to the deceased. Adapting Buddy's X-rated life into a Disney eulogy didn't leave the preacher a whole lot of material to work with.

"What can we say about Buddy?" The preacher folds his hands to his lips and looks up to heaven.

"He has gone to a better place . . . we hope."

Buddy's wife, Jane, head bowed and staring into her purse, pulls out a Kleenex and dabs at her dry eyes.

Buddy used to say Jane was so hard she could crack nuts by looking at them.

Jane has a mouth like a drawstring purse and a face that looks just a bit like a shrunken head.

When we were kids, Buddy told us she'd been captured by cannibals.

"The heathens tried to eat her," he said, "but she was so bitter they spit her out."

We believed every word of it and decided the heathens must have bitten off her rear end, because for as long as we'd known her, she'd never had one.

To this day, we still can't look at Jane without thinking about the *National Geographic*.

We finish the hymn "Take Me Just As I Am," and the preacher motions for us to sit. Jane nervously shifts from one hip to another on the pew, and the sound of bone hitting wood reverberates through the chapel like she's beating a South Pacific drum.

". . . Buddy was a good provider for his family," the preacher says.

Back in Jane and Buddy's day, there was no such thing as divorce. You fought to the death. The thirty-year war Jane and Buddy called their marriage produced three shell-shocked sons. After the youngest was born, Jane moved to the guest room. Buddy never missed her.

Buddy said she kept her bedroom door closed so the bed wouldn't thaw.

Running out of anything he can say about Buddy in mixed company, the preacher launches into his sermon on the Resurrection. Shifting restlessly, the men in the congregation stare at their watches and count the seconds until they too can rise again.

Buddy lies in an open casket at the front of the chapel. He died with a smile on his face, and nothing the mortician tried could wipe it off. If there were a TV tuned to the Dallas Cowboys and a Budweiser resting on his chest, you'd think Buddy was napping in his den.

At the rear of the chapel, the funeral director opens the double doors that lead outside. As "Nearer My God to Thee" snaps and pops over the intercom, Jane makes her way up the aisle to give her last respects to the man who never gave her any.

Suddenly, a squall of wind blasts through the door like a tempest. While the preacher swats flying carnations with his Bible, wreaths topple, and hymnals, pages flying, go skidding across the floor.

Before Jane knows what's hit her, her dress blows completely over her head. While mothers cover their children's eyes, the rest of us stretch to get a look at Jane's missing derriere.

Arms flinging, Jane's purse spins out of her hands as if caught in a centrifuge, and glossy pamphlets of every cruise Carnival offers sail around the room like confetti at a ticker-tape parade.

Chin tucked against the gale, Jane fights her way to the coffin. With as much dignity as she can muster, she stares down at the face she spent thirty years slamming the door on.

They say the longest journey a person makes is the eighteen inches between the head and the heart. As the wind howls, Jane's hardened face slowly softens. Gently, she leans down into the coffin, and just as her lips come to rest on Buddy's forehead, the lid slams down on top of her.

Chili Conundrum

Mom says she always knew Sweetie would be successful. It's her theory that a man who can spit ten thousand seeds out of a piece of poppy seed pound cake is capable of anything.

Sweetie is staring at his dinner as if there's a cockroach doing Hamlet in the bottom of the bowl.

"What's the problem?" I ask, scanning his meal for movement.

"It's chili," he says, pushing the bowl away. "I hate chili."

I'm guessing I've made a pot of chili twice a month, from October through February, since the first time I fed Sweetie. That's roughly one million bowls of beans. "Who are you?" I ask. "And what have you done with Sweetie?"

The fact is, no matter how well you think you know a person—you don't.

First it's chili; the next thing you know he's wearing black leather and a dog collar, and singing heavy metal.

"You've never complained about my chili before," I say, as I follow him into the kitchen.

"Yeah, well a guy will do anything to get fed," Sweetie says, as he scrapes his untouched bowl of chili back into the pot.

I really shouldn't be surprised. It was, after all, Sweetie's mysterious air that drew me to him in the first place. It only stands to reason that dark and dangerous men are probably picky eaters.

"So, is it just my chili you don't like . . . or all chili in general?" I feel I have a right to know if he's been eating around.

"All chili," Sweetie says, as he rummages through the pantry.

I have two gallons of chili bubbling and boiling on the stove, and the man tells me he's chili celibate.

"I had no idea," I say. "How long have you been faking it?"

"The signs were always there," Sweetie says, as he cracks open a can of Campbell's and dumps it into a pot. "You just never bothered to read them."

"And why are you telling me this now?" I ask.

"I thought it was time to take our relationship to a bean-free level," he says.

"You mean, this goes beyond chili?"

"I'm talking Mexican food," he says.

"Not my green-chili quesadillas with guacamole and black beans," I say, grabbing my chest.

"Barf city," he says.

Sweetie takes a sip of soup, spits a microscopic bit of carrot out the side of his mouth, and adds pepper.

Sighing, I push him aside and pour the soup into two bowls.

"You're not eating chili?" he asks.

"Actually, I hate chili," I say.

"You mean you've been fixing that stuff all these years because you thought I liked it?" Sweetie says, staring at me in disbelief. "Wow, that was stupid."

This from the man who's been choking it down for almost two decades.

"And what have we learned from this situation?" Sweetie asks.

"We should eat out more," I say, slurping a noodle.

I place the bowls on a tray, Sweetie hits the light switch, and we head for a another meaningful meal in front of the TV.

Down at the River

~~~

HALFWAY INTO DAVE LETTERMAN'S TOP TEN List, Lucy got it into her head to jump off the Cumberland River Bridge. Should she actually go through with it, it will most likely be the only thing she ever finishes in her life. If it were up to Lucy, she'd still be sitting in the birth canal weighing her options.

"Cappuccino?" I ask, stretching to pass the cup over the rail.

"It's from the *Texaco*?!" Lucy gags, reading the cup by the light on the bridge.

We're sitting a half mile down river from the rendering plant. The woman's about to leap into a cesspool of pig parts, and she's getting picky about her coffee?

"Hold your nose," I say. "You're gonna need the practice."

Lucy starts to take a sip, then looks up at me and frowns.

"I'm jumping off a bridge here . . . and you stop for coffee?"

Actually, we stopped to get Sweetie cigarettes. The coffee just kind of happened.

The damp air mixed with the fumes from the rendering plant has created a sort of odor cement. Perched on a girder, Lucy's starting to look a little limp, and she smells like a bag of soggy pork rinds.

Arms crossed, Sweetie leans against Mike's truck, smoking a cigarette. Meanwhile, Lucy's husband, Mike, beside himself with concern, checks the air in his tires.

You have to envy the way guys stay cool during stressful situations. If Lucy were on fire, Mike would probably be gapping the spark plugs.

"He doesn't think I'm going to go through with it," Lucy says, crossing her legs and sipping her Texaco cappuccino.

"Honey, the only thing you've ever finished was our wedding vows!" Mike yells. "I should be the one jumping off the blasted bridge!"

Rolling her eyes, Lucy bounces her foot up and down.

"Ask her about the cake decorating business," Mike says to Sweetie.

Huffing, Lucy flips her head away.

"Twenty-five hundred bucks! TWEN-TY-FIVE-HUNDRED-BUCKS!" Mike yells, stomping his foot with each syllable. "And she never even baked a cupcake!"

"He never supports anything I do," Lucy says to me.

". . . then, there was beauty college, court reporting school, real estate school, nursing school. . . ."

"Can I help it if blood makes me light-headed?" Lucy yells back over her shoulder.

"Here's a question for you," Mike says to Sweetie. "Just how light headed can an air-head get?"

"This is all your fault!" Lucy snaps. "Dr. Laura says you're an *enabler*."

On that note, Sweetie pushes himself off the truck. Judging by the look on his face, he's about to do some enabling himself. Eyes wide, Lucy grips the girder like Polygrip. Leaning against the rail, Sweetie lights a cigarette off the burning butt of the one he just finished, then flicks the spent butt over the rail.

Head between her knees, Lucy watches the glowing red dot disappear into the foggy void.

"It's a long way down, isn't it?" she says solemnly.

"You're gonna look like a peek-a-poo that gums its food," Sweetie says.

Suddenly, Lucy buries her face in her hands and starts bawling uncontrollably.

"What's wrong, baby?" Mike asks, hurrying to the rail.

"I just want to be someone you can be proud of," Lucy cries.

"Oh, honey," Mike says, melting like lard in a red-hot skillet.

"You know," Lucy sniffs, as Mike helps her over the rail, "Gina Louise says modeling classes really boosted her self esteem."

"Anything you want, my little pork chop," Mike coos.

If Only Women Could Pee Standing Up

"AGAIN!?" SWEETIE SAYS. "BUT YOU JUST WENT!"

The only woman I know whose husband doesn't give her grief every time she heads for the bathroom is Chrisy. She's married to a plumber. Leaks are music to his ears.

"Geeez," Sweetie grumbles, "your bladder must be the size of a hamster's."

By the time it occurs to a woman that she has to go to the bathroom—SHE HAS TO GO.

Compared to guys, women have a very short fuse. As fascinated as men are with our anatomy, you'd think they would have figured this out by now.

Sweetie and I are cruising across the great state of Texas, where there are two cows for every man, and bathrooms are as rare as silk boxers at a rodeo.

"How about that one?" I say, pointing at the upcoming exit.

"Nah," Sweetie says, as the off-ramp flies by, "the gas is too high."

Exactly what does a car's fuel system have to do with a woman's urinary tract? It's just a matter of time before women will be required by law to rate our miles per gallon and tank capacity.

The sun is setting on the Lone Star State, and all I can think about is how much golden sunlight spreading across the desert resembles a urine sample.

By now we've passed the last signs of civilization, and my eyes are starting to turn yellow. Eyeing my empty Dr. Pepper bottle, I start doing the math.

"How 'bout I just pull over and close my eyes," Sweetie says, already veering toward the shoulder.

Somehow the thought of dangling my derriere six inches above rattlesnake territory strikes me as less than prudent.

"How 'bout you drop your pants and sit on a cactus," I snap.

Legs tied in a slip knot, I start panting like I'm about to give birth. As far as I'm concerned we have driven past the point of negotiation.

"Stop . . . the car . . . at the next exit!" I pant.

Let's just say, the Bull's Eye Saloon will probably never be featured on *Getaways of the Rich and Famous*.

Bursting through the double doors, I slide to a stop. Beer mugs suspended in midair, a roomful of cowboys check me out like I'm a runaway calf.

Making my way to the bar, I grab the bartender by the collar and pull him across the counter.

"Restroom," I growl through clinched teeth.

Trembling, he points to a long dark hallway.

At the end of the hallway are two doors that, instead of having MEN and WOMEN on the front, have pictures of cows.

It seems to me a knowledge of animal husbandry should not be a prerequisite for using a public restroom.

By now, Old Faithful is ready to blow—with or without an audience. Eeeny-meeeny-miney-moe, and I charge through the door with the best paint job.

Apparently, it was the BULL instead of the HEIFER, because

during the stampede that ensues, several poor cowboys just about turn themselves into STEERS, as they try to zip up on their way out the corral.

"Feel better?" Sweetie chirps, as I climb back into the car.

Actually, seeing all those frosted mugs has made me a little thirsty. But I figure now is probably not the best time to bring it up.

How Does My Garden Grow? Just Ask the Neighbors

SWEETIE CALLS MY VEGETABLE GARDEN DEATH Valley, but this year, I'm going to make him eat his words. I've memorized the *Farmer's Almanac*, studied every episode of Martha Stewart, and bought Victory Garden knee pads. After extensive research, I now know when they say to add lime, they don't mean to your margarita.

"According to my calculations," Sweetie says, hitting TOTAL on his calculator, "we could buy the state of Idaho for less than you spend trying to grow a potato."

"Get back!" I order, making a cross with a couple of tomato stakes.

Sweetie has this naive notion that gardening should make economic sense. Obviously, he doesn't work for the Department of Agriculture.

"Sure, to you, it looks like a patch of gravel the road department spilled," I declare, "but this year my little field of dreams will be so lush and green, I'll end world hunger!"

Sweetie stares at me. "Have you been sniffing methane off the compost pile again?"

On my hands and knees—and elbow deep in chicken manure—I carefully lower my tomato plants into their new home.

I gave up trying to grow anything from seeds. They might as well have put cracked pepper in those little packages. Of course, it would have helped if they'd mentioned you take the seeds *out* of the envelope before you bury them.

While Sweetie may think I'm crazy, my neighbors, who are real farmers, can't get enough of me. If I plant it, they will come.

"I see she bought a hoe," my neighbor from down the road says, as he leans on his walking stick.

"You should have been here yesterday when she was trying to use it," another neighbor says, slapping his knee.

I don't mind that the first neighbor to spot me in my garden clangs a dinner bell to let the others know, but when they start parking lawn chairs in my crab grass, I draw a line in the stunted sugarsnaps.

I make a note in my *Greenthumb Gardener's Diary*: "Next year, move garden to less conspicuous location. Jackhammer up cellar floor and buy grow lights."

"You gonna grow those little deformed vegetables again?" Mr. Greensleeves asks, as he spreads a quilt on the grass.

Last year, my corn only grew three feet tall and had ears the size of cocktail weenies. I told them it was miniature corn, like you get in salad bars.

"Oh, by the way, dear," Mrs. Greensleeves says, as she passes the fried chicken, "Reverend Lewis was wondering if you'd mind not gardening on Wednesday nights. Church attendance has dropped twenty percent since you planted your asparagus upside down."

I have higher ratings than *Monday Night Football*.

Let them scoff, I smirk, as I tamp the sterilized, store-bought, premium-grade topsoil around my hybrid-hydroponically grown tomato seedlings with my patented specialized tomato tamper. They don't make baskets big enough to hold the babies these plants are going to grow!

"What's wrong with your tomatoes?" Sweetie asks, as he stares out the window toward Death Valley. "They look like somebody nuked them."

Rushing out to my garden, I stare down at the crispy leaves of my withered plants. So much for the theory, if a little fertilizer is good, a ten-pound bag is better.

It's midnight in my garden, and I'm digging like a gopher by kerosene light. On the ground beside me is a brand new six-pack of Big Boy tomatoes. As fast as I can go, I rip up my little fried green tomato plants, sling them over my shoulder and cram a new plant in its place.

"According to my calculations," Sweetie says, aiming a flashlight on his solar calculator, "your tomatoes are going to cost about twenty bucks a piece."

It's a small price to pay for self-sufficiency.

Male Math

~~~~~

In ORDER TO MAKE IT IN TODAY'S WORLD, A woman has to understand "male math."

For example, if you add up all the times men say they "did," then subtract all the times women swear they "didn't," plug in the fact that every man I know complains the minute a woman says "I do," she doesn't, you're looking at a negative number that makes the national deficit look like pocket change.

"Rumor has it," a coworker says to me at the coffeepot, "you and Gregory are . . . you know."

"Little Greggie?" I snort. "Not in this lifetime."

And not in the next, unless I come back as a vegetable.

The closest Gregory has come to an intimate relationship is downloading pictures of Lois Lane off the Internet.

"Get real," I say, blowing it off. "Who'd fall for that one?"

"Ooooh," she says, shrugging sheepishly, "just about everyone in the civilized world."

The way people love dirt, you'd think we'd use it as common currency.

Being the "sharp as a tack," "tough as nails," "go for the jugular" businesswoman that I am, I promptly go to my office, close the door, and make a long-distance phone call to my legal consultant.

"Mommie," I blubber.

"Now, now," Mom says, as only moms can, "Hold that chin up! Look 'em in the eye! Stick out your chest. . . . ?"

A moment of silence is followed by, "Strike that last order."

In today's world, along with basic nurturing skills, mothers have to do an internship under General Schwarzkopf.

"You know," Mom sighs nostalgically, "the worse part about gossip is, you didn't get to enjoy what you're getting blamed for."

I could see how that might apply if we were talking about Richard Gere. But we're talking about a guy who drinks Yoo-hoo and keeps a block of rosin by his computer keyboard.

"By the way," Mom says, "you didn't, did you?"

Moan.

There's no way to win with this rumor. If you don't deny it, everyone will think you did it. If you do deny it, everyone still thinks you did it. If you admit it, everyone thinks you're bragging.

I figure this is going to be as tough on little Gregory as me. The poor baby's teeth chatter when I stand next to him on the elevator.

"Gregory," I say, trying to break it to the boy gently, "don't get upset, but there's a rumor going around that you and I are . . . you know."

"Real-ly?" he says, wide-eyed and chewing on a rosin-dusted fingernail.

Somehow, Gregory's tone seems to be lacking the element of surprise one might expect under the circumstances.

"Greggie, you wouldn't happen to know how this rumor got started?"

Sweat pops up on Gregory like water in hot bacon grease.

Now, either the boy is lying through his retainer, or he's suddenly developed scarlett fever.

"Gregory," I say, grabbing him by his button-down collar, "keep it up, and *performance review* is going to take on a whole new meaning."

If you want to survive in today's world, you have to know the math. When a guy pads his numbers, you just have to reduce his denominator.

Strangers

~~~~~~~~~~

SWEETIE DOESN'T LIKE TO TALK TO STRANGERS, especially if they're strange. Most of my family thinks he's a mime.

"You don't wear perfume, do you?"

The older man standing next to me on the elevator has been sniffing me like a pot roast since he got on. If he inhales any harder, he's going to give me a hickie without making contact. What's disturbing is, I'm starting to like it.

Meanwhile, Sweetie has put on his sunglasses and is doing his Invisible Man routine. As the Boston Pops, piped in from a speaker overhead, desecrates the sixties, we watch the elevator light crawl up the floors.

"I'll never understand why women wear perfume," Mr. Sniffer finally says. Lifting my arm, he closes his eyes and runs his nose from my wrist to my elbow like he's smelling a fine Cuban cigar.

"Nothing is as intoxicating as the smell of a woman's skin," he sighs.

Giggling nervously, I take my arm back before he bites the tip off and lights it.

"I can tell if a woman wears perfume, even if she hasn't worn it for days," he continues.

"Really," I say.

Sweetie punches me with his elbow.

"Nausea," Mr. Sniffer explains. "Perfume makes me sick as a dog."

Sweetie taps the 27th floor button like a woodpecker.

"It all started when I got trapped on a non-stop New York to Rome flight with an Italian actress," Mr. Sniffer says. "Throughout the trip, she kept spraying and spraying . . . spraying and spraying . . ."

Nostrils twitching, beads of sweat start to rise on Mr. Sniffer's forehead.

" . . . behind the ears . . . behind the knees . . . in the curve of her arms . . ."

Mr. Sniffer makes little noises like a cat trying to cough up a fur ball.

" . . . no escape . . . trapped like rats," he heaves, " . . . spraying and spraying . . . spraying and spraying . . ."

Sweetie can't take perfume either," I say, nodding in Sweetie's direction. "That's why I'm scent-free."

Wild-eyed, Mr. Sniffer slowly returns from his olfactory flashback.

"You, too?" he asks, leaning around me to direct his question at Mr. Invisible.

"Stabbing headaches," I say on Sweetie's behalf, "like an ice pick being jabbed between the brows."

"Hmmm," Mr. Sniffer nods sympathetically.

"Sweetie says perfume should come with a Surgeon General's warning, and that samples of perfume in magazines are nose terrorism and should be against the law."

"Bravo!" Mr. Sniffer cheers.

About this time, there's a ding and the door opens on floor 17. Down the hall, a woman is running to catch the elevator. Let's just say, you can smell her coming.

Shrinking against the back of the elevator, Mr. Sniffer goes pale.

"Calvin Klein's *Obsession*," he gasps, as he slides to the floor.

"Sweetie, do something!" I say, as I loosen Mr. Sniffer's tie.

As the woman storms toward us, Sweetie calmly takes out a cigarette and hangs it in his mouth. Just as she's about to board, Sweetie flicks his Bic.

Skidding to a stop, the woman starts backstroking like Esther Williams.

"Filthy, disgusting habit . . ." she scolds, as the door closes in her face.

"Sweetie saved my live," Mr. Sniffer wheezes, as I help him to his feet.

Shaking like a leaf, Mr. Sniffer fires up a Cuban. Two puffs later, I can't see Sweetie. And as the Boston Pops plays "Stairway to Heaven," there's a faint whiff of *Eternity* in the air.

ABOUT THE AUTHOR

P. S. WALL's weekly newspaper column, "Off the Wall," is syndicated by Universal Press syndicated. She lives in Fairview, Tennessee.